GOING 12 ROUNDS
with the
Devil

Spiritual Warfare-Lesson 1

Tracy L. Pawnee Leggins

WESTBOW
PRESS®
A DIVISION OF THOMAS NELSON
& ZONDERVAN

Scripture taken from the King James Version of the Bible.

This book is a work of non-fiction. Unless otherwise noted, the author and the publisher make no explicit guarantees as to the accuracy of the information contained in this book and in some cases, names of people and places have been altered to protect their privacy.

WestBow Press books may be ordered through booksellers or by contacting:

WestBow Press
A Division of Thomas Nelson & Zondervan
1663 Liberty Drive
Bloomington, IN 47403
www.westbowpress.com
1 (866) 928-1240

Because of the dynamic nature of the Internet, any web addresses or links contained in this book may have changed since publication and may no longer be valid. The views expressed in this work are solely those of the author and do not necessarily reflect the views of the publisher, and the publisher hereby disclaims any responsibility for them.

Cover artist: D.W. Pawnee Leggins

ISBN: 978-1-9736-2727-2 (sc)
ISBN: 978-1-9736-2726-5 (hc)
ISBN: 978-1-9736-2728-9 (e)

Library of Congress Control Number: 2018905269

Print information available on the last page.

WestBow Press rev. date: 05/09/2018

Contents

Acknowledgements

I want first and foremost to thank my Heavenly Father, Jesus Christ, for the urgency and the drive to complete this work. It is only through His loving guidance and helping hand, that this book was made possible. I am an ER nurse and a modern-day Moses … not eloquent with words, not a bible scholar nor theologian, but through this book, He is causing me to bring forth His message. Praise the Lord!

I want to thank my mother, Linda Thompson, for her fervent prayers in asking God to save her children. Thanks momma. I am now a praying mother, down on her knees for her own children and grandchildren. The Lord is so good!

Now I also want to extend a warm thank you to two very inspiring women whom I have had the blessing of meeting and becoming friends with. I want to thank both Pam Johnson and Cathy Childress for giving me the encouragement and the tools to write this book. I also want to thank Bishop Lorenzo Kelly for prophesying over me. He said, "Plant your feet child. You have work to do!" Bishop has gone on to be with our Lord during the progress of this book, but I have to mention that he was the third person to confirm the initial word that I felt the Lord impress upon me about writing. Bishop Kelly was very in-tune with the Lord and I suspect that he knew what the Lord was trying to convey to me. I also want to thank my present pastor, Bishop Troy Carr for encouraging all of the congregation to," Find your place of work in the church" and for always bringing the truth no matter how hard it may seem at times. The Lord always places those in our paths who can help us in ways that only the Lord knows we need.

Not to be forgotten, my husband and best friend on Earth, Dwight. Thank you for your understanding and support during this time of needed study, prayer and concentration. I love you and thank the Lord for you.

I wish to thank my children, Zakk, Jake and Jessie for understanding that their mother is not perfect, but who love me anyway, even with all of my flaws.

This book could not be done without those who have prayed and encouraged and helped me to get it out there on the shelves. God bless you for helping me take this work forward, for God's Word will not fall on void ground and since this work is based in His Word, I know it is meant to be.

Prologue

"For we wrestle not against flesh and blood, but against principalities, against powers, against the rulers of darkness of this world, against spiritual wickedness in high places." Ephesians 6:12 (KJV, 2012.)

The first thing I must make clear is that every one of the Lord's children have been called to pray for others and in some sense, to engage in spiritual warfare but, not every person has been called to engage in the sort of spiritual warfare I am speaking of. Casting out of demons. This is a serious thing here and I cannot express enough, it is not to be played with and you are not to engage without proper preparation. This is not Hollywood and green-pea soup here folks. This is real and this is dangerous. I'm talking, your soul's destination serious and the soul of the person you are leading to deliverance-serious. This book is by no means, all inclusive. It is short and only the beginning. It is meant as a tool to assist you to take the first steps into the beginning preparation for spiritual warfare. There will be more to come, but this book is dedicated to assist the "newbie" Christian, in the basic rules of engagement.

For a long time, I would not discuss with anyone what I saw because, I was afraid people would think I was crazy. It may seem innocuous enough but the devil knew that by planting a seed of fear in me, he now had a foothold that could have stopped this book from going forward. I did talk on one occasion with my biological father and told him that I wished God would just not let me see any of these things again. I was talking of my dreams/visions/site. My father then said, "How dare you? God gave you a gift and you just slapped Him in the face with it." Great green pickles! Boy did I feel like the bacteria that lives in the scum that surrounds the cesspool. I had to really repent and ask God to forgive me for rebuking what He wills for me to have. Thank you, God, for having the patience you have.

There is a question as to whether we can actually see demons or not. I am glad to say, that not all folks can see them but for those who can, well let's just say, they have to have a strong constitution founded in the blessed name of Jesus Christ, to handle such sights. The Bible tells us of several instances as to Jesus and the apostles, rebuking demonic forces and as a matter of fact, there are over 100 scriptural verses that show us just that. Throughout this book, I will offer you the scripture to read, study and pray on for yourselves. Do not take what any man or woman tells you as the absolute. You're required to "study to shew thyself approved unto God, a workman that needeth not to be ashamed, rightly dividing the word of truth, (II Timothy 2:15, KJV, 2012.)

The Bible tells us that we have the mind of Christ, (I Corinthians 2:16, KJV, 2012) and that we would do great things, (John 14:12-14, KJV, 2012.) Now this of course, does not mean that we should ever think ourselves as equal to God, but it does serve to show us that with the anointing of the Lord, and the faith of a mustard seed, there are several feats which we can manage. That being said, let's focus on the casting out of demonic spirits.

First, we must and I repeat, must, have a close relationship with the Lord before you step into this realm. That means prayer, fasting, reading the Word, employing the characteristics required of a Christian, and the ability to receive correction. Yes, I went there. Correction. If we cannot follow the rules and allow God to keep us in line with the Word, then how in thunder, do we expect to fight the demonic realm? After all, that would count as rebellion and that is not exactly a premise for a good relationship with our Heavenly Father. This isn't 'ghost busting' television here people, this is the real thing. This is the thing that truly does go, "bump" in the night and the very thing which, if it infiltrates you, will send a person to hell. I once heard a woman ask me if I knew enough scripture to save my life and at first, I did not know what she was alluding to, but I do now. What she was saying is that my life is hanging in the balance. Without the scripture and the application of such in the proper manner, I would have no hope of ever seeing heaven. I can, however, assure you I will most certainly see the burning pits of hell because I would not have the Word of the Lord to sustain me. That really does not sound like a tropical vacation of a lifetime to me, and I don't care if there is free parking there. I use humor throughout this work because I want you to see that God uses humor with me, and that I am human just like you, but do not be deceived, the devil isn't playing and neither can we. I do believe we are living in the last days and because of that, there is not enough time to do this delicately so let's dive in!

Chapter 1

How Do I Begin in Spiritual Warfare?

Some people believe that only certain folks have *gifts,* and that may be so for some gifts, but there are those gifts that are granted to all of His (meaning the Lord's) followers if we just ask. Let's discuss the gift of discernment.

Words are formed from our thoughts, and our thoughts reflect what we feed our minds. So if we feed our minds with garbage, then our thoughts are rooted in filth, and sewage spills from our mouths. Think this is not so? The tongue is a most unruly member (James 3:8–10 KJV). Matthew 6:21 (KJV) tells us, "For where your treasure is, there your heart will be also." Your treasure must be in God and the need to win souls for His kingdom. If not, the demons will know your true motive. So you must be certain that what you do in the dark of night will be found out in the light of day. What I am saying is if you are not rooted in God, the devil will know, and you will not be able to do a thing to help anyone. Keep reading. We will talk about discernment. I promise.

Okay, so you're saying, "Yeah, all right. So Jesus could see the demon, but can a person actually *see* a demon?" Let's continue with this study.

It is true that Jesus cast demons out of people, *but* it occurred after Jesus had been baptized and spent His journey in the desert, where He actually came face-to-face with Satan himself. If we read Matthew 4:1–11 (KJV), we see that this is where Satan tried to tempt Jesus into committing sinful acts by promising Him anything that He could wish for. Satan does the same today. He will promise all sorts of false power. Just ask my son Zakk. He became quite tied up in witchcraft. I will expand on that more in a later chapter.

Jesus knew who Satan was and actually did see him, but for the most part, we are relegated to *discerning* the spirits rather than seeing them physically manifest. Thank you, Jesus! You don't want to walk through life always seeing the physical manifestations of a demon, but be vigilant and be ready. For if and when you do see them, they can certainly disconcert you, and you don't have a time-out to gather your wits.

Although we discern these entities by the Holy Ghost, there are times when a person actually does see them as well. Have you ever seen that fleeting shadow out of the corner of your eye, or seen a person's eye color change (and I'm not talking about just changing a shade of color—I mean actually changing from one color to another)? Have you witnessed the changing of a person's voice to something unnatural? Perhaps you have smelled the most nauseating of odors when you are in the presence of a demonic entity. These are some of the actual manifestations of a demon.

The problem with demonic manifestation is that most often demons will attempt to hide, and it is not until someone with the gift of discernment is present that the demon can be seen. And it is a terrible thing to behold. Some will be bold enough to speak to you. Some will hiss or clack their teeth at you, some will try to enter your dreams, and some will physically touch you or scratch you. Just remember, as a true child of God operating in the fruits and the gifts of the Holy Spirit, and with the ability to use the name of Jesus with authority, these things cannot harm you without having permission. Do *not* give them permission. One way of giving permission is by trying to wield the authority of Jesus' name without being grounded in the gospel and having that direct personal relationship with the Father. There are other portals as well, and we will discuss these later.

Now honestly, I'm glad that it is not common to see a demon. I think that would scar the psyche of most individuals on a level that even Sigmund Freud would not be able to analyze. Or maybe he would just blame the mother again. Never mind. But here's the thing: if you tell me that you see a man with purple hair and green skin and you *know* this is what you have seen, who am I to tell you that is not what you saw? Yet there are those in this world who will deny it when someone tells them he or she has seen a demon. Who are they to tell you or me what we have or have not seen?

Listen up folks: these things are real. If not, God would not have let us know about them in His Word. It is the same for witches, necromancers, fortune-tellers, psychics, and the like. God tells us just how evil these things are. I mean really, if He says, "Suffer a witch not to live" (Exodus 22:18 KJV), then I believe He means it. Now let's clear one thing up right now. This does not mean to go around killing folks we think may be witches. But we must do spiritual battle to cast the demonic force out *(if* the person is willing to let the demon go). It means that God says what He means and He means what He says. He detests sin and abhors abominations. I believe He does not lie, and since the Bible is His infallible Word, I choose to believe the entire Word and not just the bits and pieces that would accommodate my fancy or tickle my ear. I digress, so let me get back to things at hand.

We know that Satan tried to tempt Jesus in the desert. As I mentioned, Satan promised Jesus things if Jesus would only give in to him, but what did Jesus do? He resisted.

Another piece of scripture tells us that we have the mind of Christ (1 Corinthians 2:15 KJV), and I am pretty sure there is nothing wrong with what Christ perceives. I am sure He sees exactly what is there, so why, if I have the mind of Christ, would *I* not know what I am seeing?

Unfortunately, I have had a person tell me, "You can't see demons, only demonic spirits." Okay. Then my question is "Does it really matter which one you see?" After all, you are going to rebuke either one, correct? This is a man who will not serve God and has in fact practiced the occult in times past. I am thinking that the Lord does not dwell in someone who practices everything else but the love and will of God. Therefore, I am not sure how he can tell someone what God does and does not allow a person to see when that other person is a child of God. Lord, help me pray for this young man.

You may ask how I know the state of this other individual. Well, he is a close family member to me. Oh, how the devil works. If you are sensing some irritability here, I will confess I do have some righteous indignation about the subject, for I do believe we are in the last days and I do believe that Satan is working overtime; he seeks to destroy others with his lies. The question I would propose is: Are we, as God's children, working overtime for our Father to bring the truth and the light to those who will hear and accept? All right then. Onward we go.

We are also taught in James 4:7 (KJV), "Submit yourselves therefore to God. Resist the devil and he will flee." We will discuss submission later because you have to know exactly what it means to submit yourself, and that could be a sore subject with some folks. Okay, so I have the mind of Christ and He resisted the devil so *I* can resist the devil. And guess what? You can too! The Lord has given us the authority to bind the strongman (Mark 3:27 KJV) and to cast out the evil spirits. Mark 16:17 (KJV) says, "And these signs shall follow them that believe, in my name shall they cast out devils. They *shall* speak with new tongues." We had to take notice that He said "they *shall*" not "they *might*" (emphasis on might); however, there is one caveat that we will discuss in chapter 13. Again, God only says what He means. Hallelujah and praise the Lord!

Isn't God always so good to us?

Now I know you may be asking, "Well then, how do I do this?" Hosea 4:6 (KJV) tells us, "My people are destroyed for lack of knowledge: because thou hast rejected knowledge, I will also reject thee, that thou shalt be no priest to me: seeing thou hast forgotten the law of thy God. I will also forget thy children." Now you can't take just one verse out of context. If you read the entire chapter, you will see that God is talking about the sad state that the people of Israel had fallen into and His righteous anger with them. Now wrap your head around something here. We know that the meaning of the word *thy* means "your." God is actually saying, "Okay, if you want to be this way, then not only will you be erased but I will also forget about your kids!" This is how generational curses can have a portal into your life or the lives of your children or other loved ones. The thing is, Jesus Christ is the same yesterday and today and forever according to Hebrews chapter 13 (KJV, 2012) which, would also tell us that the things that were an abomination in those days, are still an abomination today and will be an abomination tomorrow. If God tells His own chosen people that they are 'destroyed' (Hebrew translation: dāmâ-to destroy; to cease; cause to be silent; to perish, be ruined, be wiped out, cut off; (Strong et al 2001) for lack of knowledge, then we as Gentiles, would also be cut off as we have been adopted into the kingdom of God and the Lord is no respecter of persons (Acts 10:34, KJV, 2012), Enough of how not to, so let's discuss how to

The obvious first step is to ask God to forgive us and to ask Him to be Lord and Savior of our life and to ask these things with a truly broken heart. If we are sincere in our asking, then the Holy Spirit will set up shop *within* us and begin working *with* us if we let Him. It does not take an hour-long speech to ask Him into our lives so please, don't think you must be a great orator to accomplish this. Go to God with you and your words of repentance. Your prayer could be something as simple as this, "God, I am so sorry for my sins. Please forgive me. Come into my heart. I want to live for you." Once you have asked this of the Lord, you then need to make sure to find a church where the pastor is teaching and preaching the truth. How will you know this? You MUST read your instruction manual, the Holy Bible to make sure that what you are being taught, lines up with God's Word. There are many Bibles out there. There is the King James version which I personally use, the NIV, Dake's study Bible and many more. I would suggest you start with the King James version and if you don't understand the Scripture due to the old English way of translation, then get a study Bible to go to for easier understanding. As you get a little deeper into the word, you may even begin using a concordance of your choosing. There are also many commentary books on the scripture out there but please, please, be careful and make sure that what you are reading, lines up with the Word of God. You must remember that commentaries are man's opinion of what the Word means and the Bible tells us that the Word is not for private interpretation.

Once we've accepted Jesus as our Lord, you must look at the need for baptism. Yes, it is necessary. Speak with your pastor regarding baptism and it's importance. Perhaps you think, or have been taught, that it is not necessary. Well then, somebody forgot to tell Jesus because He, Himself, deemed it necessary. Remember John the Baptist? Yep ... Jesus had John to baptize Him.

Chapter 2

The Fruits of the Spirit

God has the desire to have us produce the fruits of the Holy Spirit and He wants to give His children the gifts of the Holy Spirit. The fruits of the Spirit (Galatians 5:22 KJV, 2012) according to Paul, are the characteristics or qualities which God wants us to embrace in order to become more like His beloved son, Jesus. They are His qualities and characteristics and without the production of this fruit, there is no reason for Him to trust us with the more in-depth gifts of the Holy Spirit. If He cannot trust us to love one another, or to be kind to one another, then why would He put you in the path of, and try to work through you, to rid another individual's life of demonic oppression or worse, possession?

Let's look at each of these fruits.

1. Love
2. Joy
3. Peace

4. Long-suffering
5. Kindness
6. Goodness
7. Faithfulness
8. Gentleness
9. Self-control

From the top Maestro …

1. Love-the Bible is laden with more verses of love than I can count so I will allow you the privilege of studying this concept out for yourselves but I will put some of the meanings of love out here for you:

    A. Strong affection for another arising out of kinship or personal ties, unselfish, loyal, benevolent, God's agape (pronounced ah-gah-pee) selfless, sacrificial love. (Merriam-webster.com, 2017)

2. Joy-in today's times, it may be hard to find joy but the truth is, as long as we have the promise of life with our Lord and Savior, we have plenty to be happy about. That does not mean we live in a state of perpetual bliss, but we do have a reason to be happy. If that isn't enough to make you jump and shout, then I probably need to check your pulse. After all, the thought of hell is enough to make me shudder in fright. It is described as such an awful place. I think of the scripture in Luke 16:24 (KJV, 2012), about the rich man and Lazarus. And he cried and said, "father Abraham, have mercy on me and send Lazarus that he may dip the tip of his finger in water, and cool

my tongue, for I am tormented in this flame." Now, this may not sound like much to you but you have to know the background scripture. This man was a rich man whom Lazarus would have to beg crumbs from his table. Lazarus was a beggar who was laden with sores all over his body. Both of these men had passed away and the rich man was sent to hell and Lazarus was sent to the bosom of Abraham. It must've been an awful place in hell for the rich man to beg for a man who is riddled with sores to dip his finger in water and just touch the tip of his finger to the rich man's tongue I cannot imagine allowing that to happen. You would have to be in an extremely sorry state to even ask for that. Speaks volumes, huh? Oh my! I believe I would rather have enjoyed being received into the bosom of Abraham, into the bosom of peace and rest.

A. The emotion evoked by well-being, success or good fortune, a state of happiness or felicity, bliss (Merriam-Webster online dictionary),

3. Peace-what do you think of when you think of peace? I know I think of quietness, freedom from war, living in a state of harmony with my surroundings including other people, freedom from torment of my mind and most of all, freedom to worship my Lord Jesus. With all of the threats of terrorist attacks and the uncertainty of our economy, the losses of jobs, homes and other stressors in our daily lives, it is difficult to feel that peace but I tell you, in those hard times you must lift up your hands and praise the Lord! It is easy to praise in times of peace but,

it is *necessary* in times of trouble. It allows us to show God that we know He is still in control. By this walking in obedience, we will find that peace. God knows you hurt, but he wants to soften the blow and take the hurt away. Peace ensues. Philippians 4:7 (KJV, 2012), says, "and the peace of God, which passeth all understanding, shall keep your hearts and minds through Christ Jesus."

4. Long-suffering-when I think of this word, I think of having to endure something not so pleasant. Just the thought of suffering makes me hang my head, but that is not what God is saying here. He is talking about patience which this world is surely short on. Just look at all the killings, road rage and people's lack of being able to even wait their turn in the grocery line without huffing and puffing about the person in front taking too long simply because they may be using a coupon.

The Bible tells us that His ways are not our ways (Isaiah 55:8, KJV, 2012), and we must understand that His timing is perhaps slower than our 'right now' society can appreciate. You will have to learn to WAIT! Yes, yes, I know that is a foreign term in our microwave and drive thru culture, but if you are patient, and you learn to wait, the rewards are beyond anything you have ever bought at the store. Yep! Even better than that Mercedes 380 SL you always wanted, mom!

5. Kindness-again, there are too many scriptures on kindness to list here, but God speaks all throughout the Scripture regarding kindness. We see the examples of kindness that

Jesus showed all through his teaching. You know, we already talked about God meaning what he says but when he repeats things over and over … Ding-Ding-Ding, listen up folks, you might want to write this down because it's probably on the test. When He repeats something, it is most likely something to pay close attention to, and to present in our daily lives.

A. Kindness-the quality of being friendly, generous, considerate, warmhearted, affectionate, gentleness, care (Merriam-Webster online dictionary.)

6. Goodness-the Bible tells us of the goodness of the Lord. It is His goodness that draws people to Him. If He imparts this quality into His children, does this also not mean that the child of God can also win souls to the Lord because people would be drawn to us by His light? His goodness! Seems to me like that is perhaps our job down here. We should be striving to win souls for the kingdom of God. Would that be correct? I think so. Remember, people should be able to see the light of God ON and IN us and *that* is what has the drawing power. That light is the Holy Spirit within us. Just ask the moth who is drawn to the porch light. It is the type of life that we live, that many non-believers are watching and that is what they associate a Christian to be, so, would we not want to show the non-believers, the goodness of the Lord and the benefits we have just by living for God? Truly, if we are not living the life that shows God's light, then what difference is there between us and the world? Why would someone need or

even *want* to make a change if there is no difference? Are we God magnets? Are we drawing people to the Lord? Are we the porch light?

A. Goodness: the quality or state of being good, the beneficial part of something (Merriam-webster.com, 2017)

B. Good is: to be desired or approved of; fine or superior quality, virtue, righteousness, moral integrity, rectitude (Merriam-webster.com, 2017

7. Faithfulness-All of the fruits of the Spirit are needed in our lives but the truth is, this particular fruit is often rotten in today's time. We see divorce on the rise, we see people in the workplace that will stab another in the back just to get ahead, we see people come and go in the church. Perhaps we need to look at this quality a little closer in our lives. Are we faithful in our relationships? Do we deserve the trust of another? Do we deserve the trust of God? God will never let you down because of His faithfulness. When a mistake is made, the mistake is always on our end and never on God's end. The Bible tells us that He will never leave us nor forsake us (Genesis 28:15, Deuteronomy 1:29, Deuteronomy 4:31, Hebrews 13:5, KJV, 2012, and these are only a few), He will do what He said He would do as long as we are faithful in our walk with Christ. Now remember, go back to long-suffering because His time and His ways are not our time nor our ways. Patience my young grasshopper.

    A. Faithfulness: having or showing the true and constant support or loyalty, deserving trust, keeping your promises, doing what you are supposed to do (Merriam-webster.com, 2017.)

8. Gentleness-When I think of gentleness, I think of how you would interact with a small, frightened child or when trying to tame a scared animal or working with a patient in the hospital who may be afraid. It seems that one would speak softly, with kind and true words. Using soft body language rather than crossing our arms in a gesture of "keep your distance from me", using a smile and giving cause for another to feel at ease in our company. Now, I would think that this characteristic would be most difficult for men. Truly, I mean no disrespect but it seems that men take gentleness as a sign of weakness or a that is a dent in their manhood. I know this may not apply to all men of course, but I have met so many that exhibit this type of thinking, causing it to seem to be a typical belief. Now we all know that stereotyping is not correct but it just appears to be that a large majority of men seem to think this way. I guess I would have to counter that with Jesus, Himself. He was the Word made flesh. He was a man and yet, He was the epitome of gentleness. Even when He was accosted verbally and physically, He continued to be gentle. Remember in Matthew 26:52 (KJV, 2012), when one of the men with Jesus in the garden of Gethsemane, grabbed a sword and cut the ear from the servant of the high priest when they came to seize Jesus? Jesus calmly

told the apostle to put away his sword. He stated, "Put up again thy sword into his place: for all they that take the sword shall perish with the sword." The rough translation of that is: if you live a violent life you will die violently.

Now ladies, it is our turn for a little "tough love." How many of us have been irritable or even downright rude at certain times for no apparent reason? How many times have we blamed PMS or other afflictions? I know I have, and let me tell you, I was amazing at wielding words that cut. You might even say that words were my type of sword. I was a *word* ninja. Just because we are having a bad hair-day or our fellows were not particularly attentive or even if we are "hot- flashing", it does not give us the right to cut someone apart with our words or actions. All right girl-squad, let's hear the cheer ... Gentleness, Humility, Humbleness, Yea!!

9. Self-control: Ok so this one is a hard one. Period. There are several cultures who believe in the division of our being. The Chinese believe in Yen and Yang. Sigmund Freud developed the model of the id, ego and the super-ego. There are Native American tribes that talk of the "two wolves" that fight inside of each human being. The Bible lets us know that there is constantly a war inside of us between the spirit and the flesh. Galatians 5:24 (KJV, 2012), tells us, "And they that are Christ's have crucified the flesh with the affections and lusts." The Holy Spirit is telling us what is right and wrong and what should be done, whereas the flesh wants satisfaction or gratification right now. Because the flesh wants what it wants and the Spirit knows whether those things are right or wrong, the quality of self-control will stave off

terrible mistakes we may make. We do have free will so yes, you must make a concerted effort to do what is right. The world has little self-control. I will give you a personal example.

I am the oldest of four children. I had three brothers named Shane, Todd and Jason, and they were born in that order. In 1994, Todd was killed on his motorcycle and in 2002, my brother, Jason, was killed by his two best friends. BEST FRIENDS! These boys had all grown up together. They killed Jason for the sum of $8000 which Jason had received to pay for his next semester of college. Now the one boy was not a wealthy kid but the other one was very well-off which, neither situation should make a difference in any way. The wealthy kid came from a family who owned a lucrative business. He had his own Jeep Cherokee and had his own apartment, nice clothes … etc. All of this was "achieved" at a very young age and without earning it. He was handed money, and anything else he wanted. The other young man came from a very poor family. They killed my brother for a split of the money, $4000 each. Now the rich man, proceeded to take his girlfriend and other friends out to a local restaurant for dinner while the other boy took his split of the money and bought a used car. Now tell me this world is not greedy. If these boys had even a modicum of self-control, then perhaps my brother would be married today with a family of his own by now (boy have I had to bear a lesson in forgiveness.) But here's the thing, even non-believers can have an element of self-control, so what is this self-control the Bible speaks of? It is the self-control that comes only from God. We need His self-control to put away the crutches we use such as illegal substances, alcoholism, poor judgment, bad tempers and other things that menace us and separate us from God.

All of the fruits of the Spirit are much more desirable than the nine gifts, and are necessary for our sanctification in God. What is sanctification? It is the process of becoming holy. It is only through this process that we develop a clean, close and holy relationship with God the Father. Now that you understand the importance of the nine fruits, we can now talk about receiving the gifts of the Holy Spirit.

Chapter 3

The Gifts of the Holy Spirit

Now that we have repented and allow God to make us a new being, the Holy Spirit has taken up residence in our lives. It is by the Holy Spirit working through us, that the gifts are manifested so that means, they are supernatural. They are NOT of US! You have to wrap your head around that concept. It is nothing that you can do. It is only through the blessing of the Holy Spirit that we can operate in these gifts. He can manifest them at His will. They are gifts and we should always show our gratitude to God. I know that with the way the Lord has worked in my life, I have had people ask, "How did you do that?" The first thing I make clear is, it is not me that is able to do anything, but Christ, who works through me. He deserves all credit because it is He that allows me to be a vessel He is able to use. You will have to explain to people that you can do nothing on your own and that you must always work inside the will of God and that our flesh just doesn't want to be within God's will, so you have to allow the Holy Spirit to operate. Yes, I did say allow. God is a gentleman and will never force Himself on you. Please remember this statement, as we will revisit it at a later time. You must open the door and let Him in. I Corinthians 12:7-11, (KJV, 2012), we find these gifts. The gifts of the Holy Spirit include:

1. The Word of Knowledge
2. The Word of Wisdom
3. The Gift of Prophecy
4. The Gift of Faith
5. The Gift of Healing
6. The Working of Miracles
7. The Discerning of Spirits
8. Different kinds of Tongues (speaking in tongues)
9. Interpretation of Tongues

It is noted that not every person will have every gift. Some may, but more often than not, there are different gifts for different people however, that is not to say that one gift is "better" than another, or that a person with one gift is more important than a person with another gift. The Scripture above goes on to tell us that we are one body of many parts. Think about it. You may have a brain but without legs, you cannot walk or without a voice, you cannot speak. It takes all of us, working together in Christ, to operate smoothly. If you have a gift of prophecy, praise God, but I also praise God for the person who produces the fruits of the spirit and who can exhibit love and kindness. The Bible tells us to stir up the gifts (II Timothy 1:6, KJV, 2012) SO ASK HIM! Yes, you can ask for gifts. You must be walking in His will, but He loves to give things to His children. Often, we have not, because we ask not and yes, that is scriptural. Boy am I preaching to myself right now. I get so giddy as I sit here and write, just knowing that our Father loves us so much that He will give *IF* we ask according to His will. However, God is like any other good parent, He will only give if we are being "good children." If we are not, then we should be expecting correction. If we ask in any regard other than His will, He will say 'no', or maybe 'later' once we *are* walking in His will and become obedient children. If God chooses to give you a gift, don't run and don't hide. Please use the gifts as He has chosen to give you. If He takes the time to give you a gift and you don't use it, He would gladly give it to someone else who will use it.

I think about my own situation. My biological father was a country singer and he sang with several of the big-name country singers. He had a wonderful voice and I always used to love to hear him sing. Sometimes when the band would practice in the basement I would sneak to the top of the stairs and just sit and listen. I thought my father was larger-than-life. Now, I always liked to sing, but I was afraid to sing in front of people because I was worried that I would not sound good. I made it about me rather than about God. Now here's the connection. My biological father was always about himself and I never wanted to be like that. Needless to say, I rarely sang for folks. I took a gift that God had given me and I threw it back in His face. There, I have confessed it. I am so sorry Lord. I ended up having surgery on my cervical spine and the surgery caused me not to be able to sing or even barely be able to speak. I couldn't even speak in a loud voice for a while, let alone sing like I used to. I was worried that God took my voice away forever. I promised God that if He would restore my voice, I would sing when I was asked, no matter what I thought about it. Now, I still have some reservations, but I will say that God is restoring my voice little by little, and I did sing for Father's Day in 2016 with our church choir. It is better to sing His praises than to worry if I sound okay. Thank you, Jesus! So, let's talk about the gifts of the Holy Spirit.

1. The Word of Knowledge-in the book of John1:1 (KJV, 2012), we are told that "in the beginning was the Word. The Word was with God and the Word was God." The Scriptures goes on to say in John 1:14, (KJV, 2012) "The Word was made flesh."

The Scripture informs us that Jesus has always been. He has always sat in heaven with God. He is God. The Word was made flesh, and that allowed us the privilege of Jesus walking in the fleshly form on earth to teach and to preach. He actually came to this place to walk amongst us! This is another subject that is a lesson all in itself … lol. He taught us how to behave and how to glorify our Heavenly Father, and how to live in a holy manner. He taught us how to treat one another and how to love, how to forgive, and the list goes on and on. By His crucifixion he died, descended into hell and took the keys to the kingdom of hell and then He ascended into Heaven. This is when God sent the Holy Spirit to dwell within us if we would allow it. You may be asking, 'Okay, so why are you telling us that?' I tell you this so you can understand what the Word of Knowledge is and where it comes from. The Word of Knowledge is usually paraphrasing what God has told you. Remember, the Holy Spirit is inside of us now. A Word is given by the Holy Spirit for us to speak or to know how something is supposed to go. The Lord will impart something such as telling you that you need to speak a particular message to a person or persons. I will use the example of a friend of mine. She was given a word to speak to the church she was attending. Although she felt the Lord impress on her a particular message to give the church, she wanted to be in order, so she did ask her pastor for permission to speak and he allowed her to do so. She felt the Lord had moved her to tell the church to "Wake up because time is short." From what I understand the pastor himself took a spiritual spanking because as the earthly leader of the flock, it is his position to inform the church what should be going on but had, in a sense, failed to bring forth the entire truth. Of course, God's love was being preached, but the hard stuff was being left out. It is the hard stuff that God wanted His people to hear. The hard stuff that brings us into correction may be difficult to digest because we always want to think of God as love, which He is, but there are rules and rules are what keep us walking the narrow path that God has spoken of in His Word. Let's face it, no one wants to be corrected but a good parent will always correct the child when needed and just as a good parent will correct with love, so will God.

A word from God can also be something as simple as asking the Lord where did I put my car keys and the Lord impresses on you something like this, 'Well Tracy, check under the recliner' and sure enough … These are only a couple of small examples but the truth is, His word no matter how simple, has a reason. He will pay attention to what you are doing with those smaller impartations. Why would He give you some spectacular message if you won't do what He said in a smaller impartation? He will bring forth a word when someone needs it. Whether it is to relay a message, or to help solve a problem or both, God knows your needs before you even know the need yourself (Matthew 6:8, Luke 12:22-34, KJV, 2012). Now, there is the word that may come forth in the manifestation of tongues, but we will delve more into that when we come to that particular gift so please, don't put the word of knowledge away because we will revisit this some more later. The biggest issue with a word from God, is actually hearing it. God says that His sheep will know his voice (John 10:27-30 KJV, 2012) so learn how to listen for Him. Yes He will speak to you. I know there are theologies out there that say that God does not speak these days. Really? I am not sure where that comes from because His Word says He speaks and I don't think He lies about that.

2. The Word of Wisdom-Whew, this one can be a harsh one. This gift is often used in conjunction with the word of knowledge as well as alone.

You see, sometimes, God can tell you something but just because you have the knowledge of it, you may still not understand it, or even how to handle it. Okay so now that I have thoroughly confused you let me give you an example. An example could be something like you just learned that your child's spouse has cheated on your child only four days after the wedding. The first thing is, you are going to be angry but barring the fleshly anger you know that this is not right and you know that cheating is definitely not approved of by God but, how do you handle it?

Most of us would want to tell our child to kick their spouse to the curb but is that the way God wants us to handle it? Most likely the answer is no, because of what His Word says about marriage. I'm not going to argue that adultery is or is not reason for divorce because that would be a totally different subject, but I do know that God tells us a lot about marriage. Because of the heaviness of this information you have just learned about your new child-in-law, you are going to need God's wisdom to impart the word to your child and to counsel in God's will and not your own. I guarantee God's will is much better than our own and it is His will that may not only save the marriage, but perhaps the errant spouse's soul as well. I would rather see a soul saved than a marriage destroyed.

Wisdom is not something we are born with, but something we learn, and how do we learn? Well, it's by reading the Word, praying and asking what the will of our heavenly Father is. The closer we walk with God, the more He can do with, and for us. We may not have an exuberant amount of formal education, but we can gain great Bible-Smarts if we just read, listen, learn, and apply God's will in our lives. Just knowing His will isn't enough. You must apply it. Remember, Satan knows God's will and can even quote the scripture but he does not apply it.

3. The gift of prophecy-this is a cool gift, too! Paul tells us that we are to desire the spiritual gifts but most of all to desire the gift of prophecy.

When God gives you the gift of prophecy, this is a gift where God has given you word-for-word, what to say to a person (again, this means that God will speak to you.) You may be asking how this is different from the word of knowledge so let's differentiate right now. The gift of the word of knowledge is a word that is not necessarily Word for Word but the gift of prophecy will be. Because it is Word for Word, it is a good thing to write it down or record it in some way so that when you see that person that it is meant for, you will have it all down pat. If it is a very short word, then recording may not be necessary but longer words, need to be written down if possible, in order to relay His exact words. Paraphrasing is not the accurate way to handle this particular gift. In this specific situation, you need to repeat exactly what God has said. The reason for the exactness of this Word is because, usually prophecy is used to exhort or build up another individual. In I Corinthians 4:14, (KJV) we are told, "But he who prophesies speaks edification and exhortation and comfort to men." Prophecy can also be used for confirmation. My personal example is just this. I had it in my spirit that I was to write a book on how to battle the demonic realm because this particular type of warfare is what God has been grooming and using me for. I kept thinking that I am not capable of writing something on the matter because I am not a Bible scholar but, God quickly let me know that He is, and this is how He handled it. He kept impressing on me to write this book and then a sister in the Lord said, "Tracy, I can just see you writing for the Lord on your particular assignment." She was talking about how God used me to battle the demonic. I continued to think on it for quite some time and actually, I ran from God on this issue. I'm not sure where I thought I could run to that he would not be able to find me … lol. However, I started jotting things down as God would reveal to me. I was using paper and pen to record things but then, another sister in the Lord, when she found out I was writing with pen and paper said, "God says you need a computer because you have work to do." I was gifted with everything I needed in order to write. Thank you, Jesus! I thank my sister in the Lord for her obedience to the Lord because it is much easier to write more efficiently when you have a computer. You might say, 'so' but then, I was at church one day and went for prayer with this book on my mind. Bishop Kelly took hold of my face and prophesied over me. He told me to "Plant your feet child. God says you have work to do." Now if God does not speak, how would we know what He wants done? I thought I was going to fall out in the Spirit! I was so excited. God did not confirm this assignment once, but three times! Okay, okay I get it. I'm a bit of a hard-head and I guess He thought that it would take three times to get it through to me, "Get to work, Tracy!" Needless to say, a book is born. By the way, birthing is always a painful thing and to tell you the truth, this book *is* painful. The things I have experienced are not for the faint of heart and if it had not been for the fact that God allowed me to hear His will through the prophecy of others, I may not have even taken on this task. That, in itself, would've been a huge failure because God needs this information to get out there to you folks. You know, from the days of old, warriors prepared for battle by doing certain battle exercises. People would spar in the practice ring and they would even be injured on occasion. They had armor and they WORE it. After all, armor does no good to protect the body if it is not placed on the body. The armor was for protection but people still ended up with cuts, bangs and bruises. It is time to look up to heaven and listen because God is raising His warriors up in the preparation for battle. It is painful so please, remember to gird up with the armor of God! You cannot even begin to battle if you are not willing to prepare first. You can't skip steps because shortcuts will only get you, or someone else, harmed or worse. What is this armor I am speaking of? It is the armor of God and it is found in Ephesians chapter 6.

4. The gift of faith-This gift is amazing. We each have been given a certain measure of faith. We would have to have at least some faith or how would we ever trust that there is a God in the first place let alone, give our hearts and lives to Him?

I mean, if we didn't believe God exists, then what would the purpose be of living for Him? It is the small measure of faith that allows us to take the leap and live for the Lord. In order to do the things God wishes, we must grow in faith. Again, I will use this book. With the confirmation I received, it caused a cascade of faith in my life. No, I'm not saying I have the greatest faith there is, but I am saying that my faith is definitely increasing. I started by writing the old-fashioned way and I trusted the Lord would write this book and that I would have enough pens and paper and even have a publisher who would be there to help me. Because of the small increase in my faith, God went further and supplied me with everything equipment wise, that I could ever possibly need to write this work. Now because I am using this equipment, doing my reading and research, He increases my faith even more. How? Well, over time I think I am done with a particular piece in this book but He impresses on me to, 'hold up a minute' and

He starts pouring more out. He is writing this book in a way that the everyday average Joe can understand. Yep, that's for me I do not mean that in a bad way. I just know that like I said, I am not a scholar nor theologian and so I need things brought down to a level I can understand and therefore, He does. I think about my mom talking to me about Jesus and Peter. Remember when Jesus asked Peter if Peter loved him more than the rest, (John 21: 5-17, KJV, 2012)?

He asked Peter three times but if you read the original Greek meaning, the first two times Jesus use the word *agapaō* (Strong et al., 2001) which is the ultimate level of love. Peter replied that he did love Jesus all three times but it wasn't until Peter was asked a third time and Jesus uses the word *phileō,* which is a friendly or a brotherly love (Strong et al., 2001), that Peter was able to understand what Jesus was truly asking. Of course, Peter loved Jesus as a brother but he did not understand the level of love that Jesus was initially talking about so Jesus had to bring it down to Peter's level so he could understand. It wasn't just whether Peter loved Jesus or not, it was the issue of 'How much do you love me that I can trust you with my kids when I am no longer here? That did not make Peter stupid, it just made him on a different level and by the readings of Peter's work, he, certainly was no dummy. So please, I do not mean for this work to sound condescending, only for it to be understandable.

5. The gift of healing-This gift has had me stumped for years. I have seen amazing healings and I have seen others pass away without healing, so what is this gift all about?

The first thing I want to make clear is that you cannot just go up to someone and demand they are healed. God does not intend for all to be healed while here on earth. This is evident when we see strong Christian folk who have had an illness and they have passed away. Why? Well it was not God's will for them to be healed at that time. If it is His will for someone to be healed, He will impart that word to you and will tell you to lay your hands on someone and command the illness to leave and it will. It also may mean that you are to lay hands on them and pray that they receive comfort if they are not to receive complete healing. I experienced this one night when I was praying for a friend who, because of back pain was to have surgery. I was laying there in bed praying for her and God impressed on me to get down on my knees. I said okay to the Lord and I got out of bed and down on my knees and I continued to pray for her. He then impressed on me to physically go to her house and pray for her. Okay, that's when I began to argue with the Lord. I mean after all, I had just put my pajamas on, was laying down for a good night of rest, yeah right! I argued with God and said, "God, it is bed time. If I go over there this late, she will think I am crazy." He continued to move me to go but, I continue to wrestle and resist Him. Just a quick side note here, I don't advise arguing with God. This wrestling continued until 3 AM and I'm really surprised he didn't put a divot in my thigh just as he did with Jacob. I finally said, "Lord, I promise I will go first thing in the morning." He was not happy with me but did allow me to go to sleep but at 7 AM promptly, He woke me up and reminded me of my promise. I said, "Okay Lord" so I got out of bed and I called my friend and I said, "I know this may sound crazy but, can I come pray for you?" She said, "Oh would you please. I have been in pain all night." Again, I felt like the bacteria that lives in the sewers. If I would have just listened to God, and went and prayed, could she have had a more comfortable night? Probably so. Boy did I take a spiritual spanking. I got in my car and I headed over to her home and when I first got there she could barely walk. She said her pain had been terrible all night. I began praying for her and when I put my hands up to her back, it was like God just revealed what was wrong and allowed me to see what was going on inside. It was awful! The terrible twisting and curving of her spine, I knew she was in such pain. When told her what I saw, she said that she would have to tell her surgeon. She told me that at her last appointment, he had spoken to her, and had told her what was going on in her lower back which was exactly what I had been shown. Wow! When the praying was over, she was able to walk with very little pain. Thank you Lord and I am truly sorry I didn't obey sooner.

God may use the gift of healing in your life on one particular type of healing such as back pain, or cancer or even the common cold. He had me to lay hands on my grandson recently when he was feeling pretty crummy with a cold. My son said that the baby had been up all-night crying. When I laid hands on him and began praying, my grandson calmed and stopped crying and even started laughing and playing. Now I am not saying I have the gift of healing, but God chose to use me that day for that purpose. God is so good, isn't he? This type of thing is also a vehicle to manifest greater faith in us. I also do not tell you these things to build myself up because first, it is nothing I can do, and it isn't to make you go "OOOHHHHHH" because of the supernatural. It is to show you the necessity of a close personal relationship with the Lord in order to grow and to show you His power.

I believe that with the way times are going, people are not going to be able to just run to the doctor any old time. With the lack of appropriate healthcare, insurance is refusing to pay for certain care, lack of money and the increasing illnesses we are seeing, it is time to go to the great physician and allow God to heal us wholly. Not to mention the chip that they want to put in everybody's hand or forehead so that they can "keep track" of our health records. I don't know about you, but to me that sounds too risky to me. Makes me think if the mark of the beast that is coming. Just saying … I am not implying that you should go to God lastly, I just mean that it is time for the believers to actually believe that God can heal and allow it to happen if it be your destiny. So, for those of you who are called into the healing ministry, God bless you!

Just remember, if He calls you to do it, then do it because He is about to do something marvelous. Obedience is the key way we gain a greater relationship with the Lord. Not to mention it will spare you a terrible spiritual spanking.

6. The gift of miracles- This gift is the type that can cause speechlessness.

Let's say you've been called to lay hands on and pray for the cancer riddled individual and the person is completely healed! Holy buckets! Now that is a miracle but, even the salvation of the abusive, drug addict, sexual deviant or the alcohol addicted spouse is a miracle. The casting out of demons is a miracle! Jesus told us that we would do even greater things (John 14:12, KJV) and if the Lord is the same yesterday, today and always, this means that miracles were not just left to the days of the Bible. They can, and do occur today my friends. This gift takes a great compilation of the fruits and the gifts. God can manifest any gift at any time but truth is, if we cannot operate in the smaller things, how can He trust us with the greater? The greater things come after we are obedient in the smaller things.

7. The discerning of spirits-this is the bread and butter of spiritual warfare. Let us first look at the meaning of discernment.

   • Discernment, according to the Merriam Webster's online dictionary, is the quality of being able to grasp and comprehend what is obscure.

That's a pretty important point to think about. Obscure. You see it is easy to understand the things that you can see but it is those which are obscure and you cannot see, that the Holy Spirit will help you to realize are present.

We are living in perilous times and things are just getting worse. I think even the non-believer can look at the world today and know that it has gone nuts. Killings, deceit, perverseness, all of the things which God considers an abomination, are relatively accepted in society today as being all right. Again, if God is the same yesterday, today and tomorrow, then those things which he calls sin or abominations in times past, are still sin and abominations today. There is no way to sugar coat this information, people. Wake up church! Open your spiritual eyes and see what has happened, what is happening and what is still to happen. It is time to stand on the promises of the Lord. If you think things are bad now, there are only worse things to come according to the Word. It is time to stand and you can only stand if your foundation is solid. Jesus is the chief cornerstone and nothing is stronger than that.

A pretty evident example would be knowing the difference between a deer and a moose. You may say, 'Well that is pretty obvious.' Exactly. It is obvious. You are able to see the physical differences but what about those things that you can't see? We have the Holy Spirit dwelling within us and He gives us the ability to discern that which is of God and that which is not of God. In I John 4:1-4, (KJV, 2012) the Bible tells us how to discern spirits. He says to us, "Beloved, do not believe every spirit, but test the spirits, whether they are of God; because many false prophets have gone out into the world. By this you know the Spirit of God; Every spirit that confesses that Jesus Christ is come in the flesh is of God, and every spirit that does not confess that Jesus Christ has come in the flesh is not of God. And this is the spirit of the antichrist, which you have heard was coming, and is now already in the world."

The Holy Spirit that dwells within us will rise up against that which is not of God. As I said before, maybe it is just a feeling you get or an actual nauseating smell or even the actual demon showing itself. 'Whaaaat', you may be asking. Okay, there have been times when I was in the presence of a demonic entity that showed itself through a person's eyes. As I was talking with this person, I could see her eyes physically changing. Not just a shade, the way blue or green eyes may do, but an actual color change. I noted the person's body movements were not natural and as it came toward me, I made my excuses and left. I did not stay and rebuke the spirit because I, myself, was not learned nor experienced enough in this area to take on a demonic entity. I could have landed myself in the same trouble this person was in and that is why I say please, do not take this lightly. You must be prepared for it and the only way is true growth in Christ. Without the knowledge, wisdom, discernment and such, you can end up a statistic. It is not only the soul of the afflicted that is in jeopardy, but yours as well. A blind man cannot lead a blind man through a minefield safely. DO NOT PLAY with this. Do you remember when I said we would discuss portals? Playing can be a portal. It is real and it is dangerous folks.

God also gives us the ability to discern the spirits of the Angels. When we are in the presence of a godly angel, we should be calm and at peace but remember, the enemy can present itself as an angel. Test the spirits as the bible has shown us. Know who and what you are dealing with. When it is not the spirit of God, we may experience that "ooky" feeling when someone is around. That is the Holy Spirit trying to tell you, Danger Will Robinson, danger!

Sometimes, you may experience a truly horrid smell. It may be enough to make you physically ill to your stomach. Now that does not mean that every individual that has poor odor to them, are demonic. Maybe they just need a bath. There is no way to explain it. You will just know it when you are in the presence of the demonic.

Then the big one. There are times, a demon is brave enough to allow you to see it in it's true form. Yes, I have experienced this as well on some occasions. It seems that when God battles the lesser demons and conquers, the bigger ones are deployed to try to intimidate you. Yes you. They don't scare God … lol. Remember this, all demons are of Satan and the Bible tells us to resist the devil and he will flee. That does not mean it will be easy. There may be times you will do serious battle in the spiritual realm but again, this takes spiritual conditioning from God. The biggest thing to remember is, you will not be the one battling. But the Holy Spirit through you will do the fighting.

Discernment is necessary for many aspects of the Christian's life. Discernment of the spirits of course, discernment of how to use our finances to the glory of God, the discernment of situations we find ourselves in, discernment in our relationships, etc.

8. The gift of tongues-to put it plainly, this is the supernatural way of speaking a language that you have not previously learned.

He can choose to manifest tongues by allowing you to speak a language of this world such as Greek or Armenian, Spanish or Latin or any of the others. He can also cause you to speak in a language not of this world. A heavenly language. The language of the Angels. For the most part, you will not know what you're speaking because it is a language used between the Holy Spirit and God unless you also have been given the gift of interpretation. It is a personal language used to communicate with the Lord. It is intercession of the Holy Spirit on our behalf. Now, I know what you're thinking. You are thinking, "Can't God understand me when I speak in my native tongue?" Of course, He can. Or you may be thinking that tongues were not meant for us.

Okay I'm not sure where that comes from because in the Bible, it tells us different. Mark 16:17, (KJVs, 2012) says, " …They shall speak with new tongues." The Greek word that was used was glossa (Strong et al., 2001), and this indicated that the languages used would be languages that were not previously spoken by the individual. Heavenly languages. Acts chapter 2 is slightly different. Chapter 2 uses the Greek word dialektos (Strong et al., 2001,) which indicated that they were speaking in known languages but in different dialects. This way, the people who were being spoken to by the apostles, could understand what was being preached and taught that day. This is still a miracle that they were speaking in languages not native to themselves, it just wasn't the heavenly language we speak when we are praying in tongues strictly between yourself and God. Why would this even be necessary? Because there are times when we just do not know how to pray and therefore the Holy Spirit will take over and intercede between us and the Father. He will speak in the tongue He needs to speak in.

It has also been said by many pastors that I have listened to, that you cannot speak in tongues without an interpreter. The answer is yes and no. If you're praying to God in the spirit and are speaking in tongues, that particular conversation is not to be interpreted by another because it is not a word for them and God is certainly capable of interpreting His own. It is strictly the Holy Spirit interceding for you in a language that the Holy Spirit deems necessary. It is not other people's concern to be honest with you what you and God are talking about. That is no way to edify the Lord because those tongues would simply cause confusion in the church and since God is not the author of confusion, His Word will not come forth in tongues to a group of people, without proper interpretation.

9. The gift of interpretation-there are a couple of things here we need to cover. First, when we pray in the Spirit, this is the Holy Spirit interceding and taking the perfect prayer to God the Father. Sometimes we may not know what or how to pray on a situation but remember, the Lord knows our needs even before we do and because of this, He knows how to take the prayers to the Father.

The Bible asks us to pray for interpretation. This is used so that we can understand what the Holy Spirit is taking to the father in our personal prayer life, but it is also used to bring forth the interpretation of a Word spoken to the church in tongues. You have to understand that if a Word goes out in tongues and it is not interpreted, then the understanding is unfruitful and therefore, has fallen void and we know that God's word is not unfruitful nor is it confusing nor will it fall on void ground. You can pray for God to give you the gift of interpretation and this is a way to grow closer and have that deeper level of relationship with God the Father. As promised, we will now discuss submission.

Chapter 4

Please Remit your Payment, Thank You

First, let me make it clear that there is no payment you can give which will buy your way into heaven, but there are some things which the Lord does require of us. This concept is likened unto the utility companies. The utility company provides light, heat, water, etc. but in return, you must make your payment to them or they will shut the utilities off. God is the same. He will provide everything you need but you must give Him something in return. You. This chapter will focus on submission and what that really entails.

According to the online Merriam-Webster's dictionary, the definition of submission is: the act of submitting to the authority or control of another.

Control! Oh my goodness. You mean you have to let someone have control of you! Well again, God is a gentleman and will not force himself on you, so you have to allow him to have control.

The first acts of submission we learn are those to our parents. We learn what is and is not accepted in our household, what our curfew is or was, who we could and could not hang out with or who we could or could not date. We learned many rules and regulations while growing up so this is not a new concept I am bringing to the table here. It is just that, as adults, we thought we could make our own rules and do our own thing. We thought we would answer to no one that we did not wish to answer to. Seriously, the thought of being controlled is a concept that really got my goad I must admit. I mean really, how many of us said, "I can't wait to be on my own so I don't have to follow your rules mom and dad!" I know that I did. But here's the thing, God requires your complete submission to Him. He cannot work with someone who still tries to hold on to the "old man." He is looking for the person who will put the old man off and put on the new man according to Ephesians 4:22 (KJV 2012.) I realize that you cannot physically change into a new person but what the scripture is saying here, is to put away the old way of life you've been living and to put on the new, godly life He requires of us. The new man, is the life that God gives you. The holy life. Submitting to God is not weakness. No way! In fact, it takes someone very strong to say, "Okay Lord, here is my life. Do with it what you will." You are literally giving Him your life to mold and shape into something He can use for the ministry. After all, remember when we pray the Lord's prayer ... Not my will but yours be done ... We have to be willing to labor strictly in His will which requires total submission because the truth is, He does not need us to try to help him by injecting what we think is needed. That's a good way to mess things up. This will be a very hard thing for those of us who have a *trust* issue. There is no magic word I can give you to increase your trust, but I can say this, there is nothing and I mean nothing that God will do that will harm you. In fact, the book of Jeremiah tells us just the opposite. In Jeremiah 29:11 (KJV, 2012) the Lord tells us, "For I know the thoughts that I think toward you, saith the Lord, thoughts of peace, and not of evil, to give you an expected end." You see, the Lord wants nothing but the best for His children and if we will only walk in His will, He will see to it that we are taken care of in the best way.

Chapter 5

Who Are You, and What Authority Do You have?

Now that you are a child of God, have repented, confessed that Jesus is Lord and have been baptized in the name of Jesus, you may want to know something else very important. Who are you? Who are you as a Christian? Oh, how deep this goes and a book could be written on this one subject alone but, it is necessary to understand who you are as one of God's children in order to wrap yourselves around what He can do through you if, He is allowed to do so.

I think about the time when Jacob was wrestling with the angel. Jacob said he would not turn loose until he was given a blessing. Now when we read the scripture, we know that he was actually wrestling with God.

Why is it important to know this story? If we start at the beginning of Jacob's story, we read how Jacob was a liar and a deceitful man. His very name indicates a con man. Jacob had faced struggles most of his life and when this angel wrestled with him, the angel asked him, "What is your name?" That may not be a big thing to many people but it is a very important question. Here is why … God made Jacob face up to who and what he had been. He made Jacob realize that he could not go on without God. It was when Jacob fessed up and understood God for who He was, and that he realized who he, himself was IN God, that we read on to see that God changed Jacob's name to Israel. Genesis 32:28 (KJV, 2012) says, "And He said, thy name shall be called no more Jacob, but Israel: for as a prince hast power with God and with men, and hast prevailed." God then blessed Jacob in verse 29, Jacob asked the angel's name and he realized that he had been wrestling with God.

What does this have to do with you? Well it is very important to know who you are and where you have been in order to see who you can be and where you are going. You have to dig inside and ask yourself, "Who am I? What kind of person have I been?" When you can answer these things truthfully, you then know how to confess to God and ask him for forgiveness and the assistance you need but the truth is, God is not limited by your thoughts. Even if you don't think you have been in need of repentance, you can still ask God to reveal to you what you need to confess and He will help you with that. Believe me, there are none among us who are without guile at one time or another. You have to understand that once you choose to live for the Lord, what that name now entitles you to. As a child of the King, you now have become royalty and as a royal child, you have certain heir ships, certain promises and also certain responsibilities. As a child of

God, you now become joint heirs with Christ. Romans 8:16-18 (KJV, 2012) explains this.

"The Spirit itself beareth witness with our spirit, that we are the children of God: and if children, then heirs; heirs of God, and joint-heirs with Christ; if so be that we suffer with him, that we may be glorified together. For I reckon that the sufferings of this present time are not worthy to be compared with the glory which shall be revealed in us."

Jesus sits at the right hand of God. He is heir to the kingdom of God. If we are joint heirs, this means that we too, are to inherit heaven as our home. We have the privilege of being princes and princesses in the biblical sense.

The next thing to realize is that when He says that we have something, we HAVE it. He says what He means and doesn't really care to say anything he doesn't mean.

He sent His only begotten son, that none should perish but have everlasting life. Not only that, but to have life more abundantly by the way.

We have the mind of Christ according to I Corinthians 2:16 (KJV, 2012) which tells us, "for who hath known the mind of the Lord, that he may instruct him? But we have the mind of Christ." I am pretty sure that Christ has a sound mind and a good mind. With a good and a sound mind, comes good and sound practices, decisions and judgments so I'm pretty sure that the judgment of the Lord is on point. So, good minds sound minds good decisions good practices good, good, good … did I say good?

God says we have not, because we ask not. Now this doesn't mean that just because you want a Lamborghini that he will give it to you if you asked for it. Of course, it does not mean that he won't either. It *does* mean that if we are asking things, we must be asking for the things that are within His will. I don't think I really want anything he does not want for me. Usually what I want, just ends up making a mess of things anyway. God wants to give you things but you have to ask and you have to ask for what it is that is within His will for you to have. I mean, I want to go to Bora-Bora with a see-through floor in my bungalow, but so far, that hasn't happened. I reckon God doesn't feel like a vaca and Bora-Bora right now but, you never know.

He tells us to knock and the door shall be opened. Seek and you shall find, ask and it shall be given.

He does not promise that life on earth will be all rose and sparkling water, but he does promise us paradise in heaven with Him if we are living the life He wants us to live and we confess Him as our Lord and Savior.

There are literally thousands of things He has and wants for you and you can do all the things He want you to do through Him. This leads to the heavier stuff now.

Authority. We have authority in God as His child and this is a huge piece of spiritual warfare. It is this authority that we have, which will allow us to cast out demons in Jesus' name. If you want to know how important it is to know who you are in Christ and what authority you have, just read Acts chapter 19. We learned through his writing that Paul was preaching and teaching in the name of Jesus Christ. He was able to perform miracles via God working through him. He laid hands on the sick and the sick were healed. He cast out demons in the name of Jesus Christ. Others did not quite understand the magnitude of what was actually occurring. They heard these things being done in the name of Jesus so they decided they would wield the same name. Problem was, they did not understand what was required of a person first, in order to have the authority to use Jesus' name. It is noted that these people were attempting to cast a demon out however, the demon spoke directly to them and said, "Jesus I know and Paul I know but who are you"(Acts 19:15, KJV, 2012)? Demons know when you *do* or *do not* have the authority to use the name of Jesus. This is why I told you that you cannot play with this stuff because the demons will know. It was this ignorance that cost them dearly. We know this because the scripture goes on and says the man with the evil spirit leapt on them and prevailed. They ran from the house without clothing and they had physical wounds. ***Never*** try to wield the name of Jesus without the true authority to use it. It is the mightiest of weapons in a Christian's arsenal, but can be a very detrimental thing to those who are not authorized and trained to use it. Improper use can literally cost you your soul.

Chapter 6

Preparing for Battle

Now that we have the basis for spiritual warfare, we can delv into the fighting portion of it.

In a warrior's preparation for battle, he or she would nor nally don armor. Did you know that the Bible tells us to gird up with the armor of God? Yes it most certainly does. Now, this is not a physical armor such as chain mail and helmets but none-th -less, it is a Christian's armor. What is this armor you ask? Eph sians 6:10-18 (KJV, 2012) explains,

> "Finally, my brother, be strong in the Lord, and in the power of his might. Put on the whole armor of God, that way you may be able to stand against the wiles of the devil. For we wrestle not against flesh and blood, but against principalities, against powers, against the rulers of the darkness of this world, against spiritual wickedness in high places.

Wherefore take unto you the whole armor of God that ye may be able to withstand in the evil day, and having done all, to stand. Stand therefore, having your loins girt about with truth, and having on the breastplate of righteousness; and your feet shod with the preparation of the gospel of peace; above all, taking the shield of faith, wherewith ye shall be able to quench all the fiery darts of the wicked. And take the helmet of salvation, and the sword of the Spirit, which is the word of God; praying always with all prayer and supplication in the Spirit, and watching thereunto with all perseverance and supplication for all saints."

I don't know about you, but it seems to me that there are some of the fruits and gifts within this armor so without them, how can we dress for battle? The only way to put on the armor, which is our very protection, is to be living the life that God requires of us when we are His children. Developing that open-line of communication with Him so that we will hear our "orders" for battle. We must learn to read the word, employ fasting, and develop a strong prayer life and *listen* in order to receive His instructions. These are not the only things required of us.

Prayer and fasting are the pre-battle necessities. Neither, is to be taken lightly nor used as a 'drive-by' tool. What do I mean by drive-by? I mean something like, "Thank you Lord for everything you've done. Be with me today. In your name Jesus, Amen." Now you may be asking me what is wrong with that type of prayer because, I have already told you that you do not have to make an hour-long speech and that you do not have to be an orator to ask for forgiveness and have Jesus come into your life. I would answer by saying that there is nothing wrong with that as long as this is not your typical prayer. That is fine for a newly born Christian but for those of us who have been following Christ for a while, our prayer life should be much longer for there are many things that Jesus should be bringing to our mind to pray on. The Lord tells us certain things about prayer.

In Matthew 6:5-15 (KJV, 2012), we learn that Jesus' disciples asked Him to teach them to pray. Jesus answered with what is known today as The Lord's Prayer. When we break this prayer down, we see first, we are instructed to give praise to God. 'Our father who art in heaven hallowed be thy name." You see, praise comes first. We are to acknowledge His kingdom, His will to be done. We are to ask for forgiveness and then lastly, we are to ask for what we need. Again, God knows what you need before you ask. You know, we folks that are parents and grandparents, we want to give things to our children and grandchildren but the truth is, we want to know they love us and appreciate what we do for them. Think of it like this: a child comes up to his or her mom or dad and says, "I need money and I need the car keys" and that is how they constantly 'ask' for something. Now if they ask with a kind attitude, just a simple, 'Hey mom/dad, I love you. Thanks for all you do. Can I borrow the car and may I have $20 please.' The old saying is true, 'you catch more flies with honey than vinegar.'

Our heavenly Father is the same. He wants to know that you love Him above all and that you recognize His sovereignty as Lord. Remember, He already knows what you need so take the time to 'love up' on Him. He is our Father and just like our earthly parents, He too, wants love from us. After all, that is the sole reason He created Adam and Eve. He wanted that relationship, that personal relationship and He still wants that today. Think about how bad He wants this. He wants this so much that He sent Jesus to be crucified so that the damage done by Adam and Eve would be rectified and we could be restored to the Lord. Wow!

Enter into a private place and pray. You don't have to act as the hypocrites that prayed out loud, wanting mankind to hear and in fact, Jesus tells us that they have their reward coming. Why? Because they were trying to impress men rather than kneel and worship the true King. It does not matter what others think, it only matters that you do God's will. This does not mean that you cannot pray in front of others, but when you do, it does not have to be out loud unless you have been asked to lead a group in prayer. As we pray in sincerity, the Lord will begin showing you more and more which, by the way, will expand your prayer life. This means that you will spend longer and longer amounts of time praying. That is what I meant by saying I hope drive-by prayers are not your typical, every day, prayers. When you pray, take time to stop speaking and listen when you have asked something of God. After all, it is rude to ask and then not allow Him time to speak too. As your prayer life grows and you develop that personal relationship, you will begin hearing from God. You will hear him speak to you sometimes spiritually and sometimes audibly and I'm here to tell you, it is so amazing! He has spoken to me in love, authority, correction and in humor. I love to hear His chuckle. It is so warm and soothing. John 10:27, (KJV, 2012) tells us that we know His voice.

The only way to develop a relationship with someone is to talk with them. Get to know them. Ask things of them. It is the same with God. He wants a relationship with us and that means that He will have a dialogue with us if we will hear Him. Do you want that type of relationship? If not, then please, you must be told right now, that you cannot fight in spiritual warfare because you are not prepared to hear your orders. How can the military fight if they do not have their orders? It would be pretty chaotic I would think. You know, when Joshua was preparing for Jericho, he was told to march around the city once a day for six days and to be quiet and then seven times on the seventh day and to shout. We all know the walls came tumbling down but would the same result have occurred if he did not listen to the instructions? Most likely not. God spoke very specific instructions to Moses about the promised-land but when Moses did not follow *exactly* what was ordered, he was not allowed into the promised-land It is important to listen to God in order to know what He has to say.

The next thing is fasting. We have been told in the Bible that there are some things that only come by prayer and fasting. Now you may be wondering what the importance of fasting is so I will tell you that fasting is for strength and growth. It is not a method of trying to manipulate God into doing something for you. Fasting is the act of giving up food, fluids, or anything that might be taking up your time such as video games, cell phone, reading things that are not of God etc. I am not talking about praying for a Jaguar car or diamond rings or such material things that are unnecessary. I am talking about things like needing a home to live in, needing a job, or for a child who is practicing the occult and you are praying for his or her salvation.

Just as Jesus, in Matthew chapter 6 (KJV, 2012) teaches us how to pray, it continues on to teach us about fasting.

"And when you fast, do not look gloomy like the hypocrites, for they disfigure their faces that their fasting may be seen by others. Truly, I say unto you, they have received their reward. But when you fast, anoint your head and wash your face, that your fasting may not be seen by others but by your Father who is in secret. And your father who sees in secret will reward you."

When we fast, you cannot go around with a grumpy face or bellowing about how your tummy is empty or thinking about when we will be allowed to have our next meal or wondering about who is online in social media. Fasting must be undertaken after you have asked God to lead you in your fast. What you are to give up … Food, fluid, cell phones or all of the above. How long are you to fast? Is it just a day or is it three days, is it 36 hours or just from sunup to sundown each day? Yes, there are instances of much longer fasting but I would suggest talking to God and let Him tell you and then carry it out. Smile, pray, praise and obey. See the mighty mountains that are moved. Remember the mustard seed? There are several scriptures that can assist you in learning about fasting and since there's somewhere around 40 or so, I will allow you to study fasting for yourselves. There is no way in one book, I can teach you everything, but God inspired the perfect manuscript. It's called the Holy Bible. Beyond that, He can speak to you and guide you further so please, understand that this book is not to make you ready to go out and fight spiritual warfare. It is simply to tell you what is coming and that you must be prepared for it. This writing is to tell you how to *begin* the preparation. We have to learn to walk before we run. It gives some of the examples that I have been through, but your experiences may be different and I am sure that they will be. I emphasize again that you cannot read this book and think that you are prepared. This book is simply meant as the beginning lesson to teach you what must be in place in order to battle in spiritual warfare. This book is to reiterate that the relationship you have with God is the only way to prepare for the coming onslaught of the devil.

Chapter 7

The Battle

You have repented with a broken heart, asked Jesus to be your Lord and Savior and invited the Holy Spirit in your heart. You have found a church that is preaching and teaching the truth and you attend every time you can. The Bible has become your daily ritual instead of the daily newspaper (I'm not saying don't read the paper), and your prayer life is growing by leaps and bounds and you can have a two-way conversation with the Lord. You are bearing the fruits of the spirit and you are operating in the gifts of the Holy Ghost. You have now donned your armor and have learned a little about fasting. Now, you have to ask God what His will is for you as a worker in His Word. Okay, so you say He has told you that you will be fighting in the realm of spiritual warfare. You are going to be fighting the demonic. You believe that you absolutely know this beyond a doubt. I would throw this in then ... Talk with your pastor or someone who is strong in the

Lord and can help you pray on these things because I'm here to tell you that you are going to need the constant covering of prayer.

The next thing is for you to understand the difference between oppression and possession.

1. Oppression, according to the online version of the Merriam-Webster dictionary, it states that oppression is:
   a) the unjust or cruel exercise of authority or power
   b) something that oppresses especially in being unjust or excessive exercise of power
   c) a sense of being weighed down in body or mind

I will give you a situation that happened to me one evening when I had gone into my bedroom to go to sleep. My husband and children were upstairs in the living room and our master bedroom was downstairs in the basement. I was alone downstairs, or so it seemed at first. I laid down in bed and as I was starting to doze off, I could feel a presence that was not friendly to say the least, and when I opened my eyes I could see fire at the foot of the bed and up around the sides. I could feel a presence pressing down on me to the point that I could not speak, yet I could see nothing except for the fire. I tried and tried to yell out for my husband but could not even get out a whisper. I was terrified and I knew what this was. Even though I was not living for God at the time, I knew who and what was bearing down on me. It was a demonic force and it was straight from the pits of hell. Now, I knew who Jesus was but I did not have a personal relationship with Him but let me tell you, it was the beginning of one! In my mind, I called out the name of JESUS! Immediately, the presence was lifted and the fire was gone. I did not have the experience nor the power to fight these things but Jesus did! It was this that caused me to start pursuing Jesus. I have fallen off of the path a few times, but to His credit, He picked me up, dusted me off and set my feet straight again. Thank you, Jesus for your love and mercy! He knew what He could do with me even if I didn't, as long as I would just let Him work. Remember, the Lord is a gentleman and as I said before, he will not force Himself on anyone. I want everyone to understand that I did not stay in the situation because I wanted to. I was in it because I had a portal open and it was strictly the grace of God that I had survived it with my soul intact.

This force had not entered into me, but was bearing down on me and that is the difference between oppression and possession. Oppression was the bearing down of the presence whereas possession is the actual entrance of an entity into your body. I truly believe that if I had not called on the name of Jesus, possession was on its way. Oppression may not be as easily assessed as possession unless there is a certain level of discernment present. God allowed me to recall lessons taught in church when I was young and this allowed me to call on Jesus. It also caused me to give my life to Jesus, obviously not without stumbles and falls but through learning, the falls are becoming less.

I would like to talk to you now about actually seeing the spirit and no, I am not talking about the Holy Spirit. I am talking about seeing the true form of a demonic spirit. God has, for some reason, allowed me to see these things on several occasions. I have seen them hiss at me and clack their teeth together and look at me through the most evil of what I think is supposed to be eyes. Normally they show themselves to me in black cloak-like apparel but not always. One was flippant enough to be wearing a blue pin-striped suit (Insert a big-eyed emoji here … lol) and top hat. Their eyes have ranged from an iridescent blue to the blackest of coal. Their skin has presented itself as a pasty white. Not like a human albino's skin, but even more so. Perhaps translucent is a good word to use here.

2. Merriam-Webster online dictionary (Merriam-webster.com, 2017) defines possession as:
   a. The condition of having or owning something
   b. The act of having or taking into control
   c. Control or occupancy of property without regard to ownership
   d. Something owned, occupied or controlled
   e. *Domination by something (as an evil spirit, a passion, or an idea)*
   f. A psychological state in which an individual's normal personality is replaced by another
   g. Self-possession

There are so many ways that the demonic will be revealed so let's look at the obvious. Possession.

Seeing them always shocks me. As we have discussed before, there are times when a demon will allow you to see it through someone's body. The eyes are what I have seen first. The color will change from one color to another. Then the body movements of the individual become very abnormal, almost robotic and also in very unnatural positions. This is a case of actual possession and I am here to tell you, it is a little disconcerting. I cannot say the demon will present itself in the same way each time you face one but the truth is, they are not very original. They will use just enough truth to try to draw you in but the Holy Spirit is the one that gives discernment and the discernment is what gives you the knowledge that something is not correct. Discernment is the bread-and-butter of the warrior who is battling in the demonic realm. Discernment, is the Holy Spirit telling you to 'Buckle up Buttercup because this ain't right.' It's God's way of letting you know that you are in the presence of evil. By testing the spirit, you will know exactly where the spirit is from. If the entity can tell you that Jesus is the Lord and Savior and came to earth and died for the sins of the people and went to hell and took the keys to the kingdom of hell and is the only way into heaven, then well yeah, it is probably an angelic spirit from God. *IF* the entity denies these things, then we know that the spirit is demonic and was sent from the father of lies, Satan himself. We will not be discussing the angelic spirits in this book because to be honest with you, I'm not worried about them for our particular subject in this book, but it is the demonic spirit that calls for action.

If you have not developed the type of walk with God that I have already told you about, then your only action is to leave, quickly. Do not hang around and try to battle this thing. You cannot do it. You may be saying, "Well you did in your bedroom." Let me make this clear. I was extremely fortunate that Jesus heard me and I truly believe it was only because He knew that I would become a warrior for Him eventually. I can only fall on my face and thank Him for the grace He showed by coming to my aid in such a perilous situation. He did not have to.

If everything is in place and you know you are to battle, then the next step is dependent on the position you are in. If you find yourself face-to-face with the demonic, then it is to wield the name of Jesus. How? Like this, ask God to protect you from the evil that is present and then firmly state something to the effect of, (and I will use the example of the spirit of Jezebel here) 'In the name of Jesus, I command you, spirit of Jezebel to leave and to return to hell where you belong. You have no authority here and you cannot stay.' No, you do not have to use these exact words but you will need to state that it is in the name of Jesus that you are demanding the exit of the demon. Sounds simple, right? Not so much. If there is any doubt in you, or if you are not truly living for God, the demon can tell. Again, I bring the Scripture back of the sons of Sceva and the high priest who attempted to cast out a demon. Remember, the demon spoke directly to the "priest" and asked, "Jesus I know and Paul I know, but who are you?" The men were physically attacked and the demon prevailed upon them. Notice I used the example of Jezebel here. You may be wondering how I can use a name. This is the thing, many times, God will give me the name. There are other times, He has not given me a name. Nonetheless, the demon will know if you are under the authority of God, and if you are not, this is an example of a portal right there that can allow the demon into your life. The demon will know if you have the authority to use the name of Jesus. It is the only name that can cast out an evil spirit. We have already talked about names and authority so you must be walking in that authority and have the 'ok' to use it. The name of Jesus is copyrighted you know … lol.

If it is a situation where someone has called you and has asked you to pray or to come over because there is 'something in the house', then I tell you to hit your knees first. Enter into prayer with praise and let God know that you know who is really in the driver's seat. Repent of any sin that you may have committed and ask God to reveal any sins that you committed that you are not aware of and then repent of those as well. Gird yourself with the armor of God. Know your scripture. Ask God to miraculously bring the scripture to you that you may not know or remember but that could help you in this particular battle. Ask God to go before you in this battle and to protect you from all evil. Ask Him to allow you to be the vessel He needs you to be and to help your faith and obedience to be what He wants it to be. Pray for the deliverance of the person and ask to be the one to take the Word to the situation. God will tell you if you are the one for the job. Do not step outside of what God tells you. If you are the one, then I would suggest praying in the Holy Spirit. Yep tongues. When we are praying in tongues, it is the heavenly language between the Holy Spirit and God the Father. This means that the perfect prayer is being sent through the direct line to God on your behalf. The Holy Spirit is interceding for the situation and for things you may not even know need interceding for. You need to spend as much time on your knees as God deems necessary.

Okay, so someone has called you over to their house and God has given you the 'ok' to go. I use the same procedure once I go into the house but once there, the process is a little deeper. First thing's first. Pray that God place a hedge of protection around you and those with you. You will then need to ask God to go before you, as you enter the house. I would suggest that you again, pray in the Holy Spirit. There are times, the demon may only give you a *feeling* but there are times when you will see it, smell it and/or hear it. Again, you will command the demonic entity to leave in the name of Jesus. Command it to leave the person/dwelling and go back to hell where it belongs. Here's the thing, you may command it in the name of Jesus *but* if the person who is living there is not a child of God, then they have left a portal open to allow the demon to come back into that person or the dwelling. Attempt to lead the person to Jesus if they will hear you. If not, then there is not much you can do. There is also the issue that a person may not wish to release the demon and we will discuss that later. There are times where you will know the demon's name. This becomes important when you are dealing in the demonic. They do not want you to know who they are because that gives you further power to discern not only who, but how many, there are present. By knowing their name, you have further dominion over the situation.

Movies have shown that it may take several days, weeks, months or years, to get a demon to be cast out but that is not what the Word of God says. Jesus spoke once. Yes once. The true authority of God does not give the demon a choice to stay. There are times I have prayed for hours but that was the end of the situation. It did not take days. Now, back to the demon. Notice I said the *demon* doesn't have a choice however, a person does. The demon leaves when it is told to by the authority of Jesus Christ and the demon has nothing to say about it. There are scriptures all through the Bible that support this. You can study in Matthew 4:10, 8:16, 8:32, Mark 1:34, 39, Luke 4:35, 41, 8:29, 11:14-19, 13:32 (KJV, 2012). This is not an all-inclusive list but it will get you started. There again, is one caveat to this and it is discussed in Chapter 13.

Chapter 8

Portals

When I talk of portals, I am talking about the places or things that give the devil his legal rights to enter into your life. Portals are an infinite number of things and include things such as an ungodly life, disobedience to God, practicing the of the occult, pornography, certain things such as particular movies or TV shows that you watch, unfaithfulness in your relationships, music and the list goes on and on. It is literally anything which draws your life away from God.

When you choose to live in an ungodly life, it means that you have chosen to live of the world. God tells us that we live *in* the world but we are not to be *of* the world (John 15:19, I John 2:15, James 4:4, John 17:14, KJV, 2012). What does that mean? It means that although we live in this world which is filled with sin, we must strive to live and practice God's will. We must be obedient to Him and His Word. We have to live in this world because, how else would we take the message of salvation to people if we are not in the world? Be not *of* the world is simply just that. We are not to partake in the sin of the world, but to lead people out of that sin. We are called a "peculiar people" after all (I Peter 2:9, KJV, 2012), "But ye are a chosen generation, a royal priesthood, an holy nation, a peculiar people; that you should show forth the praises of him who have called you out of darkness into his marvelous light." We should be the porchlight folks.

Peculiar … this would indicate that we are people 'owned' by God. You must understand that at the time of the King James version of the Holy Bible, peculiar meant a sort of property. I know, you are thinking that peculiar means something like an odd duck. Well yes, if we are not living as most of society lives, we probably are considered odd, but that is not exactly what the Bible is saying. God is calling us 'chosen'. If I choose a blouse and purchase it, then I own it. Do you not think God owns you? He purchased you with the blood of His son, Jesus! Remember our talk about submission? Umm hmm.

Disobedience leads to repercussions. Now I am not saying that each act of disobedience is going to cause a portal to open but I am saying that if you cannot receive God's correction and put that correction into practice, you will eventually leave the devil, room to move in.

To practice the occult is to most certainly open a portal immediately because God speaks against such witchcraft. It is an abomination to God and remains just such. People who practice Wicca would tell you that they are practicing white magic or that they are trying to be naturalists. I can tell you this is a lie straight from hell. God says, "suffer a witch not to live," according to Exodus 22:18 (KJV, 2012), and He did not add the exception for the white magic witches. Again, let me clarify that this does not mean to kill those who are practicing the oocult. After all, this would be against His commandments but, it does mean that we have to battle spiritually for the person afflicted. It means to put the demon to flight straight back to hell in the name of Jesus!. The Bible tells us that we cannot add to, nor take away one word from the scripture and this is found in various places throughout the Bible such as Deuteronomy 4:2, Deuteronomy 12:32, Proverbs 30:6, Revelations 22:18-19 (KJV, 2012). Remember, God says what He means. This takes me back to the books of Exodus and Leviticus where God had brought the people out of Egypt and gave very specific instructions as to the building of his tabernacle of the congregation. He was so specific, right down to the type of wood/materials and how many of each thing and where to place it. So, you can bet if God takes time to say it, He means it.

The occult is a wide variety of things. It is practicing witchcraft, playing with things that call forth spirits such as the Ouija board. You may scoff at that, but when people die, they are asleep in Christ and not walking this world nor can they be called back to this world so just know that whatever you are "calling back", is not of God. Remember the story of Lazarus and the rich man again? That rich man wanted Lazarus to come and just give him a drink of water from the tip of his finger but, the rich man was informed that Lazarus could not cross that barrier. It is the same now. When someone passes on and has been placed in the grave, you cannot call their spirit back. These spirits that enter through those portals are what God calls *familiar spirits*. God specifically states in Deuteronomy 18:10-12 (KJV, 2012), that it is detestable to God:

> "There shall not be found among you anyone who makes his son or his daughter pass through the fire, one who uses divination, one who practices witchcraft, or one who interprets omens, or a sorcerer, or one who casts a spell, or a medium, or a spiritist, or one who calls up the dead. For whoever does these things is detestable to the Lord; and because of these detestable things the Lord your God will drive them out before you."

I would say that this is a pretty sore spot for God. If He finds it detestable, then you should not be doing it. Period. There are reasons as simple as, if you do, you put yourself and others in peril so think about what God has to say about speaking to the dead the next time you think about whipping out the Ouija board. I'm not kidding. What makes me sad is how the game business markets this seemingly innocuous 'board game'. They use a child on the front. A child! For Heaven's sake does that not seal the adage that if the devil gets our kids then he has the future? Parents, I implore you to teach your child and stand against the use of these objects. The Ouija board is not the only object that can be used for the occult. Stones, crystals, runes, tarot cards, automatic writing, astral projection, channeling, horoscopes, magic, numerology, psychics, palm reading, divining rods, and séances are a few of the 'tools of the trade' but by no means is all inclusive. All I can say is stay clear of each of these things. I know from close experience that these things are dangerous. I will explain more in the next chapter.

Pornography, this one speaks for itself really. If you have to look at sexually explicit pictures or movies in order to have some sort of satisfaction, then there is a serious problem here. God tells us about our relationships and that our desires are to be for our spouse. He tells us about lust and that it is the same as adultery which is something that he despises. Our sexual appetites are reserved, ladies, for our husbands and for you men, it is your wife. I wish to make that clear because no, God does not recognize same-sex marriages. That is also an abomination in God's eyes. Here's a prime example of being in the world but not being of it. I live in a world that says we need to be tolerant of same-sex marriages but I say NO! God's Word speaks against it and for me to say it is okay, well that is not upholding God's Word. By the way, homosexuality is not something that a person is born with. God is the only one that can give life, and he does not create an abomination. People choose it. Sorry scientists, you will never convince me otherwise. We know that if something is not of God, then it is of Mammon and since God does not approve of homosexuality, then it must be of a demonic spirit. Yes, I just went there. You don't believe it? Then you need to read your scripture. What does God say about homosexuality? A lot. Leviticus 18:22 (KJV, 2012), tells a man not to live with a man as he would a woman. He calls it an abomination. Leviticus 20:13, (KJV, 2012), goes on to tell us that they shall be put to death. Now, I am not saying that we have the right to go around killing homosexuals because that would be against God's commandment that we are not to kill. It also does not mean to mistreat a homosexual. It means that God will exact that judgment and that homosexuals will not see heaven, but instead, will burn in the pits of hell. It is our job however, to bring the Word, the truth to the homosexuals and to pray for their deliverance. I realize that may make me unpopular with some folks, but here's a secret … I'm not here for a popularity contest, I am here to bring the truth. I stand on God's Word, His Word is truth, in His Word He calls homosexuality wrong. I told you, I truly believe we are in the last days and I don't have time to dance around the demonic realm. I call it out for what it is and wish to expose the devil's wiles so the people can go to God for forgiveness and deliverance. Yes, I believe that since homosexuality is a demonic force, a person can be delivered of it. I say these things not in malice, but in love for the souls of those who are afflicted by demonic forces.

The things we are watching, the movies on television, can be a portal for the devil as well. What do I mean? Well, just as I explained before, what we feed our minds is spilled out on our tongue so if we are filling ourselves with garbage, then garbage will come out. If you are watching things such as the occult, you will probably find yourself eventually looking into it in one way or another. If you are watching violence, then you may find yourself unable to practice the fruits such as love, kindness, gentleness. If all you are watching is smut, then you will find yourself daydreaming or thinking of those things. Think not? Then asked the woman who is constantly reading her non-Christian love stories and finds herself wishing her husband was like the character in the book.

That leads to a feeling of un-fulfillment and that leads to feelings of resentment and that can lead a person to further destruction such as lusting or affairs. I am not saying that this is what happens to all folks but it does happen. Please be careful.

It seems that people always want to know what I actually see. It's like they need gory details or something, but you know, we must be careful of the demonic forces that are obvious as well. You may ask what I mean by that. I mean the every-day, demonic forces that are at play right in front of us that we seem to ignore. Can you think of none? I can think of several. Let's look at a few of those right now.

We are going to go back to homosexuality for a moment. I am sure that people are aware of homosexuality. This is not of God which means it can only be coming from one other source. Lucifer. Yes, homosexuality is a demonic force. I say this because only God can give life and we know that God does not create an abomination. So no, children are not born with a tendency for homosexuality. If you have questions about that, then I would suggest you read John, Romans, Hebrews, Leviticus and the many other books containing scripture on the matter. God calls homosexuality an abomination. He did not tolerate it then and He does not tolerate it now. This leads us to understand that no, people are not born homosexual because if they were, then God would be creating the very thing He hates. Since God is the one who gives life and He does not create an abomination, that means people are influenced by demonic forces to take on that type of a lifestyle to pervert the life God intended for them. I just saw a trailer on television the other day regarding the gender issues today. That trailer was trying to tell us that we should not only accept homosexuality, but now people are trying to say that it is okay if you don't want to be a male. You can just have a sex change or that if you don't want to be a female … It sounds like a 'change' like you would change clothes. I am appalled that the world has fallen into such despair! I have news for you, if God intended for you to be a male He would have made you one. I don't care if people say that they knew they were a male/female when they were young and that they were only trapped in the wrong body. Do you really think the devil does not mess with our children? Of course, he does. If he can get our kids, then he has the future. Think about it. Okay, so you want to ask about the hermaphrodite/intersex person. Yes, I reiterate that God does not create an abomination and intersex individuals are no more an abomination than the child born with Downs's syndrome or any other birth defect. Ok so why would God allow birth defects? We must go back to Adam and Eve. There was no deformity when they were formed. God created them in His image. A perfect pair. It was not until sin entered the world, when Eve took of the fruit of the tree of knowledge of good and evil, that we started having issues with health. We can see this in the decreased length of lifespan in the generations that followed Adam and Eve. We see the diseases that plight our world and of course, birth defects. Without going into a lengthy discussion regarding the study of genotypes/phenotypes, it is safe to say that the intersex person has defining characteristics. Both men and women have some traits of the other sex. Look at the female who develops stiff hairs on her chin and neck or look at the man who has enlarged breast tissue.

This does not change them into the opposite sex. In the intersex individual, there are many things that must be looked at in order for the true gender to be ascribed. The whole of the individual must be examined. The genitalia, the hormones and the DNA/chromosomes of course, are some of the composite materials we have to look at. It is only with great diagnostics that we are able to determine if the child is male or female. If you have further questions on this matter I would suggest you pray on it and talk with your pastor about it but do not choose what *you* want the child to be at birth. It has been proven that about 80% of intersex children have had the wrong sex chosen for them without the proper diagnostics first. Now, we have just created homosexuality. How do you say? Because if you have a male and you have chosen for him to be a female and that female has been taught to date only men, you have now caused your child to be homosexual. Oh man, this issue can get really deep and I am not here to do a class on it so please, seek the Lord first and guidance from your pastor if you happen to find yourself with an intersex child.

Abortion. We know that God gave Moses the 10 Commandments. One of those Commandments was 'Thou shalt not kill.' Science tells us that in order for something to be considered alive, it must have cell division and replication (I remember that from middle school. I'm so proud ... lol). Here's a little anatomy and physiology 101 for you. When you become pregnant, cells immediately begin to divide. The baby begins to feed on the nutrients the mother takes in. So, we have life the moment conception occurs. There is no other way to slice it, no other way around it. Calling the baby, a 'fetus' does not change the fact that unless you bred with something non-human, you are carrying a child. And just as a side comment, yes, the Bible does speak against bestiality. Abortion kills that child by stopping the life God created. No more cell division, no more feeding on nutrients, no more nothing. Period! You can try to frost things over any which way you want but murder is murder. God spoke against it so again, what force is out there that makes us commit murder? It is not of God so once again, we are at square one. It is demonic in nature. God certainly would not place it upon your heart to desecrate a commandment that He gave. It is not rocket science here folks.

Violence has broken out en masse and we can see this in the school shootings, police killings, killings of Christians in areas of the world that are non-Christian countries, rape, beatings, substance abuse and etc. You know, I have said it once before, God is peaceful and he does not wish to gain your service by force. He is a gentleman and will not force himself on you. Now, He will use force to clean up a situation. I think again of Sodom and Gomorrah or when Jesus overturned the tables in the temple because of the money-changers that had corrupted His house but again, He does not force you to accept Him. At your choice, He will allow you to go to hell for not accepting Him although it breaks his heart. He sent His son to die for everyone. That is just how much He loves you.

Suicide. Oh my, the rate of suicide has escalated so high. According to the online site for the American Foundation for Suicide Prevention (ASFP, 2017), 44,193 Americans die every year from suicide. That is staggering information. These statistics are just for folks in American so you know that the world count is extremely high. For every suicide, there are 25 attempted suicides. What is the deal! What is causing more people to want to take their own lives? What could make a person feel so low that they think they can't get up? Can you say, 'psychological scars'? Now, maybe we can see how saying negative things to/over someone can impact their lives. People will use this however as a means not to convey the truth of God. We live in a society that wants to be politically correct. I couldn't stand having the blood of anyone on my hands, let alone a suicide because of something I may have said or did to that person but that being said, I will never pervert the Word of God for anyone. The devil loves it when someone takes their own life, because he has won that person for his hell. Now, when we look at the statistics of who kill themselves, again, the American Foundation for Suicide Prevention statistics make me want to cry. It says that men are 3.5 times more likely than others to commit suicide. I live in South Dakota where rate is 20.57 suicides per every 100,000 people. Oh God help us! (Anon 2017) states that the teen suicide rate is four times higher on our Pine Ridge Indian Reservation then across the entire nation! I see this firsthand as I do work in an ER that is situated right in between two Indian reservations. Our children are dying, why? Because the devil knows if he gets our children, he has the future. We talk about loving folks with an agape love, well, I see people caring for the people in other nations and that is a great thing, but please, don't forget the very people in our own backyards. Why are we not on our knees, interceding for people who are plagued with suicidal thoughts/ideations? I know there are some who do pray on it, but if our rate of suicide is increasing, then we are failing somewhere which means devil 1-Christians 0. You know, the Satanic church is now trying to get itself into the after-school clubs programs. That is correct. Google it. https://afterschoolsatan.com will give you a bit of information to start. That organization is claiming it's right to be in our schools. It brings me back to one woman who was able to get prayer out of the schools because the Christians sat back on their laurels and did nothing to fight as a whole body. We assumed that it would never happen but it did! There is a time to fight and it is time now. Will you join me in telling Satan, "No! You cannot have my children! You cannot have my spouse! You cannot have my family, now, in the Name of Jesus Christ, get thee back to hell!" We cannot allow Satan to get a hold of our families.

One of the biggest demonic forces/portals I see today is the issue of ISIS. Yes, I do believe they are a demonic entity, using deadly force in the name of their god, Allah, oh my goodness, that is scary stuff. They are beheading Christians and trying by force to take over nations. God is a gentle God, He is a jealous God and He will clean up this world when the time comes but I'm here to tell you, that God tries to show love first and shows mercy to those who accept His calling. I recently watched a DVD series on ISIS and its relationship to the end times according to scripture. Talk about the demonic, whew! We know Ezekiel, Daniel, Revelation and Zechariah are all prophetic books about the antichrist which is a huge demonic force right? He is going to make a way for the beast, and that my friends, is a demonic force that you cannot withstand if you are not living God's Word. I beg you to study what is going on in our world today using the scripture as your syllabus, for it tells us that the spirit of the antichrist is already here.

Our psychological scars are another portal. Yup, that's what I just said. Our psychological baggage can be an opening for the devil. I am not telling you anything you don't already know but, sometimes we may forget a little. You see, the things in our past have hurt us. Things like our parents, siblings, friends, and of course, our intimate relationships, can create that weak link. That's all the devil needs in order to wreak havoc on your life. He will take that one thing, that hurtful thing and use it against you to make you weak, and try his best to cause you to fail. Perhaps a parent who has told you that you are not good enough will cause you to constantly be afraid of failure and truly, that can cause self-sabotage because you won't step out on faith to find that actually, you CAN fly with God's help. Or let's look at that partner who no longer wants you because you have gained a little weight after having children, or the man who no longer has a six-pack stomach and perhaps has lost a little or all of his hair. The thing is, those superficial things, can cause some not-so-superficial scars. It hurts us to our core when people are cruel to us. Yeah, the devil loves to use the spirit of offense to get to us. It causes us to feel less than what we are. It causes defensiveness which in turn, may lead to hurting others. Oh man, can you say, 'domino effect'? You might wonder what this has to do with fighting spiritual warfare. Well I'm going to tell you what God said to me. He said, "Be careful what you pack in your spiritual suitcase Tracy. You may not like what you take with you." It's time to let that baggage go and quit hauling it around. If we can't let go and allow God to heal us, then the devil has something to use against us and you cannot afford to have anything the devil can use against you when you are doing battle. Don't give that creature any weapon against you. Do you remember the scripture in Isaiah 54:17 (KJV, 2012), that tells us, "no weapon formed against you shall prosper." Well if we lay our trust in the Lord He will fight our battles but you cannot wallow in self-pity. You have to actually turn it over to God to get rid of it. Don't give the devil any weapons to use. You might as well just forget trying to battle with him if you're going to give him a loaded gun against you. God redeems us and makes us whole. The father of lies will try to make that seem as if it were not so. By giving him weapons to use against us, you have told him that you believe him! The first spiritual warfare you need to be involved in is your own! Go to God and ask Him to rid you of those feelings of inadequacy, hurt, defeat, etc … If you cannot battle for your own life, how can you battle for another person? It reminds me of what Bishop Kelly once said, "Ok, so have a good cry one time but then get some gumption. Roll up your sleeves and get to work! Stop rolling around in it!" Gumption. I like that word. According to online Merriam-Webster's online dictionary, (merriam-webster.com, 2017) it means,

    a.   courage

    b.   common sense

    c.   confidence

    d.   initiative

I think that gumption is a good characteristic of spiritual warfare warriors. It is not to say that we are the ones who alone, are strong enough to battle the devil and his demonic realm, but it takes courage and confidence in God's Word, to … get this … allow God to use us. Umm Hmm, I said *Allow*. We have to allow Him to use us. If we are willing to submit to Him, then He can use us to battle for His children. It is He, that does the warfare, but it is through us that He chooses to operate.

OK …

So, stop looking for the head-spinning, vomiting green-pea soup, Hollywood junk and look at what's around you today. If you cannot discern those demonic forces and fight against them, then how in thunder do you expect to stand, when you DO see an ugly entity? Simple, you can't. At least if you *see* it then you know that it is there and we can see the horrible things going on around us today. If you cannot employ the gifts that God has for you, you will not be able to withstand what is to come.

It is more frightening to think of the enemy we cannot see. If you cannot discern, you don't even know it is there and that is dangerous. It is stealth that the devil uses to infiltrate a person. It is sly, little by little, piece by piece for the most part. It is worse than anything the movies could ever cook up. For those of you who have said, "Yeah but I just wish I could actually see what they look like." Why? What would you do with that knowledge? Do you think you have the authority of Christ to rebuke it? You can have that authority if you are God's child *and* if that is the way God chooses to use you, but you cannot choose it yourself.

I think about the two witnesses who are able to call down judgment in the end days. They preach with such power and authority that they can honestly call down miracles of God! Don't know about you, but I am still working to become that strong in my Father, the Lord God. Hallelujah and praise God! I just want to jump and shout at God's majesty. Thank you, Jesus, thank you, Jesus! Yes, praise Him out loud but do it for His glory and not the approval of others. Let me ask you something. Do you raise your hands and shout God's praises or do you sing your hymns, listen to the sermon, nod your head every now and then, and then go home after you shake a few hands with some of the folks? Don't be afraid to praise God! If King David can dance before the ark, then I surely can let people know who my God is and how I love to show Him how much He means to me. I am nothing without Him. It is easy to praise when we are on the mountaintop but harder to praise we are in the low places. What does that have to do with this book? It is as simple this, if you can't show God that you know He's 'got this' when you are in the low places, then how do you expect God to trust you with the souls of others? How can God trust you to rebuke the demonic when the soul of another is at stake if He can't count on your praises to Him no matter what the situation is? Oh! I am preaching to myself!

I must admit, I am both excited and terrified of what is coming. I am excited to know that the prophecies must come full circle for the end of times and for us to finally have rest in heaven, and those prophecies have already begun folks. I can imagine what it will be like just spending our days singing God's praises and just loving Him as our Father, face-to-face. But on the other hand, I know what He has allowed me to see on earth and I know that it is nothing compared to what is coming down the pike. I pray that God continue to give me His strength and courage because I know my own flesh will fail. The spirit is willing but the flesh is weak, (Matthew 26:40-43, KJV, 2012.) In the garden, Jesus was telling his disciples to stay awake, that something terrible was coming and He knew that they could fall into temptation. Even Jesus Himself, asked His father to take away "this cup" but, was willing to allow the flesh to die in order to do His Father's will. Are you willing to die? No greater love hath a man than to lay down his life for another, (John 15:13, KJV, 2012.) Yes, that day is coming. That is the demonic force I NEED for you to understand. There is coming a day when your life will be required if you are going to stand for God. Can you willingly give it or will you fold? You want to talk demonic, then let's go there. How about your child or your grandchild? If they say that you must renounce God and take the number of the beast or they will kill your child, or your grandchild, do you have the strength to say, "I love you son/daughter/grandchild, and I will see you in heaven" as you watch them take the head from your babies! That is the thing that is coming and that is the strength you must have. Think it isn't going to happen or even happening now? Well, ISIS has made it clear on more than one occasion exactly what they think of Christians. They have taken the heads from those who do not want to renounce God and convert away from Christianity. Do you have the ability to stand in the face of that adversary and keep hold of God to matter what? Remember, the devil roams about seeking whom he may devour. The thief, not but for to steal, and kill and destroy; I am come that they might have life and have it more abundantly (John 10:10, KJV, 2012.)

I realize these things seem pretty radical but truth is, a radical time is at hand. We have to gird up with the armor of God. We have to have the Word etched into our hearts. There is no other way to stand my friends. Perhaps we should not start by standing. Perhaps we should start by kneeling. Kneel in front of the Lord and give Him your life. Do this, and no one can take your life from you. Not even the thief. Your flesh may die, but your soul will soar with the angels when the time comes.

Chapter 9

Experiences

I'm going to share with you some very up-close and personal experiences that God has used to groom me for my assignment. Probably one of the most intense, is the story of my oldest son, Zakk.

My son knew that God was working with me and that He allowed me to 'see' certain things. My son, decided he wanted that kind of gift and he sought it out from the occult. Zakk, became very tied up in witchcraft. He explored the tarot cards and runes and other such things. I did not know at first that he was tied up in this stuff until one day, he walked into my house and I could see that he didn't seem 'right'. God spoke to me and told me that Zakk was using witchcraft. I confronted him by saying, "Son, I want you to sit down. I know that you are practicing witchcraft." I think his eyes were about to pop out. He sat down and we talked about what was going on. He let me know what all he had been doing and that a coven had actually contacted him about becoming their head warlock. He had moved beyond the tarot cards and was actually practicing astral projection. He began to cry and said, "Mom, when I look in the mirror, I can see him." When I asked what he meant he told me that he could see a demon laughing at him in the mirror. He said he could see the horrible eyes and the jagged teeth but the worst was yet to come. He told me that the demon told him that 'now he had him.' You may be asking why I didn't see the actual demon. Well, all I can tell you is that God let me know that it was there but He spared me the horror of seeing it in my own son. Thank you, Jesus! I knew that I was going to go into battle, and not for some small-time imp, but that I was going to battle for my son against some big guns. I prayed and God showed me that my son had several things to do. One of those things was to rid himself of the tools he was harboring in his home. My son was in agreement and he was terrified to say the least. I told him that I would go with him but he would not let me go. I think he was afraid for me although I knew I had someone on my side who could handle anything. Zakk, however, did not let me go with him. I told him to call me if he needed anything and as soon as he left out of my door, I hit my knees and pleaded for my son's deliverance. My phone rang and when I answered all I could hear was my son screaming, "They won't burn! They won't burn!" I told my son I needed to keep praying. This mama prayed until I thought I was going to sweat drops of blood too. Finally, my son called and said, "They're burning!" When he got back to my home, I told him that God had intervened for him and he needed to make a decision about serving God. Now, usually I can see a demon or demonic spirit, but in this case God spared me. He let me know about it, but He chose not to show it to me. Perhaps He knew how bad it would hurt. I really don't know. All I can say is thank you Jesus, for sparing me at least the pain of seeing it. Now, my son did not immediately go on to serve God. He forgot what God had done for him but God chose to remind him. My son was not resting well and he continued to see 'forms' that he knew were not of God. It tormented him. Needless to say, this mother and my own mother, kept praying for his deliverance. I can tell you that God is ever faithful. My son is now a child of God and serves Him with a willing heart. Praise you Jesus! Not only is my son in church, but he has a wife who also is learning about the Lord and they take my grandson to church to learn. The Lord is so awesome.

This story is not only unique to my son, but I also have a daughter who would not serve God. She was in for a rude awakening. One night, my husband and I were already asleep and the phone rang at 11:30 PM. It was my daughter and she was terrified. There was something in her home. It had thrown pictures off of her walls at the baby while the baby was lying on the couch. Thank God, they did not hit my granddaughter. She sent a picture to me and God allowed me to see four forms. Two ugly creatures, a woman and a wolf. I prayed over it and called my daughter back. I began to tell her what I could see and then I started praying in tongues. Thank you, Holy Spirit, for your intervention to the Father! He knew what I needed to pray and He interceded with the Father on my daughter's behalf. As I was praying, the phone became very static-y (is that even a word …

lol) and my daughter later told me that as soon as I started praying in tongues, the phone cut me out but when the prayer was over, she could hear me again. I know that Satan was trying to keep her from hearing the prayer and was trying to scare her. He did. I told my daughter that I needed to get off the phone and that I was going into battle for them. I knelt down and began to pray. Again, the Holy Spirit interceded and went to the Father on my behalf, for my daughter and her family. I do know that I asked Jesus to "Go before me" and as soon as I did, I saw the brightest, most beautiful sword come down in front of me. It came down from the right to the left and it stayed like that. Bright and beautiful. As I walked, I could see a tunnel. It reminded me of the dank dungeons you would see in an old movie. It was wet and cold. I could see those four entities above me. Two on either side at the entrance to the tunnel but I wasn't afraid. I knew Jesus was battling this. It seemed like it took no time at all really. And at the end of the battle I could hear Jesus say, "It is done." When I got up off of my knees, it was 8:30 in the morning. It had been about 8 1/2 hours of prayer! 8 1/2 hours but it only seemed like minutes. My daughter had left her apartment right after the first phone conversation. Later when I talked with her, I told her what I was shown and she then told me that my 3 1/2-year-old grandson had told her something. He had told her that a man "walked backwards" onto his bed. He told her that the man had very blue eyes and a tongue that "went like this" and he described what a snake's tongue looks like by using his little fingers. He told my daughter that the man had fingers "like this" and he held three fingers in a triangle. He told his mother how the man told him that he was going to take him into a tunnel and take him home. My grandson told his mother that this thing had actually picked up his baby sister and said if my grandson did not go with him that he would "snip-snip-snip" and "eat" he and his baby sister. He then went on to tell his mother how the dog had jumped on the man and began fighting him and then he, himself, began to fight the man. To this day, the dog has very clear puncture marks on his back. They are in the form of three points shaped as a triangle. My grandson also had scratches on his back. He told his mom that there was an old woman there that called herself, 'mother' and that she changed into a wolf. Now, how can a three year almost 4-year-old, come up with these things and how did I see them in my prayers before he told us these things? Only God was able to allow me to see what my grandson had seen. Oh, that poor child! Bless you, Jesus, for your protection of the children!

In another instance, I was called by a friend one evening about a person who was having some problems in his home. He said there was something in his house. When my friend was on the phone with me, I could hear the man say, "Test her first." That immediately made me mad because I was always told not to test God, and since God does the work and not me, it is He, that they would be testing and not actually me. Whew … I Hope that made sense. I could hear the sweetest, gentlest of chuckles and then God revealed to me to take the test. I said, "Lord?" He just chuckled again and impressed again for me to take the test. I told my friend, we will call her Susie for anonymity, I said, "Susie, give me just a minute." I got down on my knees and started praying and the next thing I knew, I was seeing the interior of a house.

I saw the colors of the walls and the furniture and even saw the decorations. I began to explain to "Susie" what I could see. Mind you, they had me on speaker phone so both could hear what I was relaying to them. The next thing I know, they told me to come over. Since I had never met this person, I did not know where he lived so my friend came after me. The rain was pouring so hard and it was cold outside. Anyway, when I got there, I spoke briefly to the man about the Lord. He was not all that receptive, but I then began walking through the house and praying in tongues. I'm sure that probably flipped him out as well ... I walked into what was probably meant as a spare bedroom but was being used presently as a storage area for a few boxes. The room was very cold and somewhat dark but there was enough light that I can only say was from God that allowed me to see a form in the back, upper right corner of the room. It was hovering and hissing. I demanded in the name of Jesus Christ that it leave and go back to the abyss where it belonged and it immediately flew down and out of the room. I followed behind it and it flew literally, out of the house. When it was all said and done, I turned around to find the man very pale. He spoke first and said, "I don't know what you could see, but all I could see was the brightest white light around you." I then explained that it was the light of God and that the Holy Spirit is the one that made the demonic spirit leave. I then went on to explain that although the spirit was gone for now, it had the ability to return if the man did not choose to close that portal by living for God. He hung his head and said that he did not believe in God but that he knew he saw "something." I told him I would pray for him and I left. I left knowing that God had shown this man exactly what type of power He has and exactly what He *can* do if the man would only allow it. I do not know to this day what happened because he moved away and my friend and I no longer run together because of lifestyle differences but I pray for them both, that they will find God.

Another occurrence happened when a dear friend of mine who is a fellow sister in the Lord, was talking with me. She was having spousal trouble. As she began telling me the trouble, I felt God reveal to me that it was the spirit of Jezebel. I relayed this to my friend. A few days went by and then one day, she started telling me about something that had been scratched on to her window. She then showed me a photo of her window and what appeared to be an organized form of writing, but the thing is, the writing was in between the panes! She invited me out to her house and showed me the window. The writing was still there, but there was also a very heavy feeling present. I went through the house praying and anointing with oil in the name of Jesus. I then went outside of the house and began walking towards the building that was a workshop. I prayed and anointed the building and continued walking towards a storage building that was used for hay and feed. As soon as I walked in, I could feel the presence of the spirit plaguing this couple. As I walked up to a landing, I saw it. It presented itself as a beautiful woman. She was clothed in fine array with her hair up and adorned with some sort of hair jewelry. Her hair was topped with a head-piece and the hair that did hang down, fell in ringlets. She truly presented herself as beautiful however, God let me know who and what she was and as soon as I called her name and began to pray against her, the wind picked up and was blowing my hair and I saw her come toward me. She grabbed my throat and began to squeeze. I planted my feet and grabbed onto a wooden crossbeam with both hands and prayed even harder and then I called her name again, 'Jezebel'. I began rebuking her in the name of Jesus Christ. She literally shrieked at me and disappeared. I then began to walk the property and placed anointed prayer cloths all over her property. There was a place I came to that was so pretty. It had these two huge conifer trees growing on the sides the gravel 'walkway' I guess you could call it. It was this place that I felt was a playground for evil. It happened to be situated by the window that had the strange markings inside the panes. I prayed and placed a prayer cloth there as well. I instructed my friend that she must walk in authority and bind these things from her home. I am thankful to say that the trouble between she and her hubby started getting better and there have been no further disturbances at her home.

There is another instance I was faced with while at work one day. I was at the nursing station and I could hear a patient having a conversation. Now, this patient had Alzheimer's, and her daily verbiage was mainly gibberish. Anyway, on this particular day, she was having a literal conversation which was two-sided. I thought maybe someone had stepped in the room to see her so I got up and went in the room to check. She was alone and all of a sudden, her head turned toward me in a very unnatural way, and she spoke in a voice that was demonic to say the least and she said, "You are going to die." I immediately put my hand up and stated, "in the name of Jesus Christ, I command you to leave and go back to hell." She simply dropped her head and went back to fiddling with her fingers.

There are other cases of the same sort of demonic shenanigans that I have dealt with, but the thing to remember is, it is not me nor you, but it is Jesus that does all the work. I am not capable of doing anything like this on my own. If it were not for Jesus, I would be a casualty of war. Thank you, Jesus!

Chapter 10

Renewal

You must also know that this sort of work takes a huge port on of your emotions and energy. There are times you may wonde why you were chosen for this type of ministry. I can tell you the you must continually go to God for renewal. Isaiah 40:30-31 KJV, 2012), tells us, "though youths shall faint and be weary, and the young men shall utterly fall: but they that wait upon the Lord shall renew their strength; they shall mount up with wings as eagles; they shall run, and not be weary; and they shall wall and not faint." Ephesians 4:23-24 (KJV, 2012) says, "and be ren ewed in the spirit of your mind; and that you put on the new man, which after God is created in righteousness and true holi ness." There are many more scriptures which refer to the renewing of our mind. I would reiterate that as children of God, we have the mind of Christ. That means that no matter how tired you may think you are, you have a solid mind. A clear mind, and a ren ewed mind. Remember, even Jesus was feeling a little overwhelmed in the garden of Gethsemane. If you read the Scripture, you will find that Jesus asked God to deliver him from having to die but he said, "nevertheless, your will, not mine be done." He was sweating blood. BLOOD! Now that is a serious issue to be on your mind in order to sweat blood. There is a condition called hematidrosis which is literally red sweat. It is caused by the blood vessels in the sweat glands that rupture under cases of extreme stress. This causes the blood to leak into the sweat glands and to come out in the sweat. Now, I don't know about you but I have been through some really stressful situations and not once, did I sweat blood although I thought I might. So yes, you will have times of extreme fatigue when battling in the spiritual realm but I'm here to tell you that Jesus is with you every step of the way. Step back, breathe and remember who is truly doing the battle. I promise you, Jesus has your back.

This is another reason why it is important to be covered by the prayer warriors. You will need your gas tank to be refilled so be ready to accept that you need help.

Chapter 11

Order

I cannot stress enough that you must be walking in God's will. You must learn what working in order means. God demands order in His workers.

When you are under the guidance of a Holy Ghost filled pastor, you will need to talk with them about what you believe is your calling. You will need to sit under the tutelage of your ministerial staff and make sure you have the covering of your pastor and most of all, of God. You will need the covering of prayer of the saints. This is working in order. Do not be offended if your pastor tells you that you are not ready. Your pastor, if working in order as well, will hear from God and will guide you in the correctness of order. If they tell you that you still have some learning to do, then take that as a blessing and work on it. Raise your hands and praise the Lord! He has just saved you from a terrible thing by showing you that you are not ready. If you take offense or feel slighted, then I would recommend you work on your pride because that is most certainly standing in your way to God and God speaks about pride in a negative way … in at least 25 verses. My favorite is Proverbs 16:18 (KJV, 2012) "pride goeth before destruction and a haughty spirit before a fall." A Holy Ghost filled pastor will only tell you what you need in order to do this work the right way. There are many things you will need to learn before you can even begin taking on the demonic realm. Why do I keep mentioning a Holy Ghost filled pastor? I truly believe it is the person who has the Holy Ghost driving their life that can help guide you to a Holy Ghost filled life. If the Holy Ghost is not residing in you, please return to chapter 1 and begin again. You will need to learn the Word including the things such as tithing, prayer, praise, correction and many other things that I cannot fit into this book without writing another installment so please, seek the face of God first and He will reveal to you what your work is to be, as well as providing you with the tools you will need to complete your task. He will not send you into a situation blind because he does not want you to fail. He does not call the equipped. He equips the called. According to Hebrews 13:21 (KJV, 2012), the Bible says, "make you perfect in every good work to do his will, working in youth that which is well pleasing in his sight, through Jesus Christ; to whom be glory forever and ever. Amen." Philippians 2: 13 (KJV, 2012), tells us, "for it is God who works in you, both to will and to work for his good pleasure." So again, if He has called you into this type of ministry, He will see that you have the tools to do the work.

It is also worth informing people that not any particular type of ministry is more important than another. We are ALL part of the body and it takes all parts working together in the will of God to create this body. God doesn't have a one-armed body you know. He is perfection and therefore, His work is perfection. I have seen people who think they are superior because they have a particular gift in the ministry but I would ask, is it more important to have a right arm or a left? Exactly, they are both just as important. Yep, you need both to tie your shoes. He will not let you go out there to do a half-brained job. The scripture in Philippians 4:13 (KJV, 2012), tells us that we can "do all things through Christ who strengthens me." This does not mean that you can 'choose' spiritual warfare and then God will say, "Ok." It simply means that we can do whatever God has called us to do and with His strength, we can accomplish a complete work.

Chapter 12

Brass Tacks

If you are a little disappointed in the fact that I haven't told you some magical spliel and arm waving to fight the demonic, well, I'm sorry. Jesus did not sit down and dress himself in fancy arraignment and pull out a book and take days to remove the spirit. He spoke. He commanded the spirit to leave and it did. Again, He did not give it a choice to stay for days on end, waiting for someone who had authority to make it leave. Now, I will reiterate that He does tell us about prayer and fasting. These are necessary staples for all of God's children including the warrior involved in spiritual warfare. It is not to make us weak, but it causes us to grow stronger in the Lord. It is this strength that you will need when you do finally face a demonic force. It is the strength that will allow you to speak something like, "The Lord Jesus rebuke you. In the name of Jesus, I command you to come out. Return to the abyss where you belong." This is not the phrase

I am telling you to speak, I am just saying it will be something of this kind. It just happens to be the way God moves me and causes me to speak when I come face-to-face with one of them.

You will find, as time rolls on, there will be more and more need for deliverance ministries. It is, unfortunately, a topic that is avoided and even evaded by a lot of the ministerial folk out here. They are preaching the love of God and don't get me wrong, that ministry is sorely needed, but I am pleading with those established in the ministry, please don't lead others into believing that after being saved, it is all sunshine and roses. Please, you are responsible for preparing your flock for the things to come. Too often, congregations are at the mercy of sermons that simply tickle their ears and tell us of all the good things that are out there, but, often are left to fend for themselves when they have not been properly prepared for the evil of this world. If we are to believe every word that God has written, then we must believe even the not-so-nice things that are coming down the road. As the devil works harder and harder putting in his overtime to win souls for hell, we have to work overtime to win souls for the kingdom of God. As the playing field becomes fraught with perils of deceit, we are the only vessels of light to help guide the lost to the Lord. The only ones who play by the rules of righteousness.

I am about to say something that will most likely offend others. I am sorry if you are offended but I am not sorry why you are offended. It is necessary for me to tell you that because the world has become so self-centered, so self-involved, that we have adopted a "whatever feels good" attitude towards life. We are told that we are to tolerate all religions, sexual preferences, behaviors, and all manners of ungodliness. I'm here to make my stand, I do not believe all religions are correct. I believe that those who walk in God's word are correct but outside of that, I believe you're walking in a lie. I do not tolerate the "whatever feels good" attitude because unfortunately, the body is ruled by sensation rather than rules. Morality is whatever you make it these days. No, I am sorry but it is not! It is that simple. Now for tolerating homosexuality, sorry, but I cannot in good conscience, say that it is okay. God says it is an abomination therefore, I cannot preach a homosexual into heaven with flowery words. These demonic forces are out in full effect but I choose to stand on the Word of God. I will not become complacent about how the world chooses to accept the devil even though they may not realize it. I will speak the Word. I will always worship the one true God and will never deny that His son, Jesus died on the cross for my salvation and the salvation of everyone that walks this earth if we just accept Him. Call me a fanatic, I really don't care. You may say that I am a hater, no, I love you and that is why I tell you these things. I will not tell you a lie about how you can live in whatever way compels you and that you will still be on the fast train to heaven. I am here to tell you that the devil rules this world and unless you get off that train, you are on a fast track to hell. No mincing words here. I refuse to be religious. Religion simply means that you are faithful at doing something. Well, I guess you could say the devil is religious after all, about making people believe the lie he is feeding you when he tells you that you can do whatever you want and still be saved. If that were the case, Adam and Eve would still be in Eden and Lucifer would still be in heaven. You see, the devil makes people believe that the Christians are mean and intolerant because they speak out about the wrong of the world. He attempts to make you believe that he is the right way because he is so accepting of you and doesn't make you feel bad about yourself. Well, I have read the end of the book and it says that every knee shall bow and every tongue shall confess that God is exactly who He says He is and He will toss the devil into hell for eternity along with all those who follow the devil. It will break God's heart to send anyone to hell and that is why he gave an "out clause" but you have to take that escape and live it.

It boils down to this … I would rather believe in God and live the way He instructs and find out when I die that death is the end and there is no God, rather than to live the way the devil says I can, just to find out that when I die God does exist, and it is too late for me to do anything about it.

Chapter 13

Those Pesky Poltergeists

I have made it clear earlier in the book that God uses a lot of humor with me but, there is nothing humorous about spiritual warfare. It is faith in-the-raw. It is scary at times and most of all, it is the literal battle for the soul of another. No, we cannot fight alone. It is strictly God that does the battle, He just uses us as a willing vessel.

I will address the issue of why some spirits just won't go. It is simple. People just don't want to let them go. The person enjoys the sense of power that the demon gives them, albeit a false one. Remember my son? He had a sense of power but we know that this is not real power and that Satan doesn't give you anything but only takes. A person has to want deliverance for it to occur. Remember that God is a gentleman I will not force Himself on anyone. He gave us free will and we have to want to have Him in our lives for Him to be able to do anything for us.

I will also tell you that you have to be ready with answering the non-Christian with the truth. Even some non-Christians believe in spirits. They just do not understand the modus operandi of them. What does this mean? Well, when a non-Christian asks how to get rid of a demonic entity, you have to tell them the truth. They can't.

Now, I am about to tell you something that just breaks my heart. My own story.

I am married to a wonderful man … most of the time … lol. For the most part, he is good and in his own way, he loves me. But, there are times, just like all other couples, I believe him to be the most self-centered, selfish and mean-spirited individual I have ever met. I have prayed for this man and asked God to change him but, it has come down to this, I had to ask God to change *me*. I had to ask for the grace to handle his meanness. His moods. His anger. I am not perfect at it yet and at times, I just don't want to speak to him when he is like that but, God speaks to me and reminds me of the horrible life my husband has went through. He reminds me that I don't know what kind of work He is doing with my husband in private.

My husband has lived a life that most people can only see on some sort of drama-filled television show. Yes, I know, we all have some sort of drama in our lives but truly, my husband went through things no one should ever have to suffer. He has lived through a living hell and is still standing. He suffered an abusive childhood, one where his father thought it funny to put beer in his bottle just to make him go to sleep when he was a baby. Where they had him drinking with the family by the age of 10.

A life where he was beaten for who knows what reason every time his dad and stepmother drank. My poor mother-in-law tried so hard to get my husband when he was a little boy but you must understand, my husband is Native American and it is no easy feat to take a child from the "Rez." Anyway, my husband grew up fighting for everything he had. Hiding food so he could eat, going for days without food, living in a car with his dad for a while. A stepmother who hated him and beat him. Siblings who hate him (except when the car breaks down and they need him to fix it for them) and a multitude of other things, (Oh God, help me to show them your love.) The worst however, is the prison time he has done because of his stepmother. She and his father and others were drinking and my husband got a call that his little sister was in the hospital so hubby rushed over to the reservation hospital and there was his stepmother, pointing at him and telling an officer, "He did it!" My husband was 19 years old and had no idea what was happening needless to say, my husband had a public defender who did nothing to help him and he therefore, did 10 years in federal prison as a 19-year-old kid. Now, you may say, "Well he deserved it!" Then I would have to tell you that his stepmother apologized to him just before she died for the lie but, it did nothing to ease my husband's anger. Now my husband is afflicted with a living entity that eats at him spiritually.

Anger. It is a terrible spirit when used in the wrong way. Now, we all know there is righteous anger but for the rest, anger is a living entity and it destroys people. It will eat you alive and, if you let it, it will rule you and it will kill you. My husband to this day, suffers with this. He has talked about it in church, he has called elders to pray for him when he is having a bad time but the bottom line is this, he needs deliverance from it. Deliverance only comes when the heart is ready to let God have it all. My husband stated, "I just have a problem giving all control away." He says it reminds him of being in prison and the things he has seen happen in there. He is hyper vigilant at times and just *knows* someone is giving him a "mean look." Slightest traffic infractions of another driver just put him on edge. Now you may say, 'well there are a lot of people who have that problem. They need psychiatric help!' Yes, they need the great physician because secular docs can only give "tools" to help you deal with the issue, but it is only God who can take that spirit away. You must be willing to give it away and my husband is not willing at this time. Now, I know God is working on him because there have been some good changes. I have spoken to him about praying for his family and the need for forgiveness. He tells me that he understands this but is just not able to come to that place as of yet. I just need to be patient and let God do His work on my husband, and this leads to the spirits who just won't leave.

You can fast up, pray up, read up and all the things you are supposed to do. You get a call for someone who is dealing with an evil spirit. Pray for protection and you go to 'drive that spirit out in the name of Jesus!' but it won't go. WHAT! But Lord your Word says … Yes, His word says, but you must understand, there are some people who like that false sense of power they have when this spirit of anger is in control. They don't want to relinquish control so they refused to let the spirit leave. Remember, God is a gentleman. He gave us our own free will (hint … that is why you must ask Him what His will is for you) and therefore, will not force Himself on anyone. No, not even the demonic-filled person. That person has to want to be freed. They have to be willing to let God in. God cannot abide in the same house as mammon. That means that God can't live in you if you want to allow a demon to remain.

These may seem like very simple principles but it is not as easy as it sounds. The road to spiritual warfare will be filled with potholes the like which you have never seen. It will drain you and sometimes make you feel like, 'what's the use' but I tell you what the use is … the soul that is delivered and is now a child of God. Your new brother or sister in Christ! That is the use. The day you do not mourn for those that are headed for hell, that's the day I would ask, "Do you need deliverance for yourself?"

I have been under great spiritual attack lately. It has come from all sides and sometimes it felt like I was drowning. I found myself asking, "Where is God?" I mean, He chose me for this assignment of spiritual warfare but I couldn't see the light for all the darkness. It wasn't until I was talking with a Christian friend of mine and she said, "Tracy, do you think that all these attacks are Satan's way of trying to turn your focus away from God?" Now that may seem like the obvious answer and indeed it is but, have you ever heard the phrase, 'sometimes you are too close to a situation to see it for what it is?' That is me, I am in the middle of this book and I know Satan does not want it completed because there is at least one person, this book is intended for. That person is getting ready to become a mighty warrior for God and this book is God's 'lesson 1' and Satan can't stand it. He is doing everything he can to stop this book. He has attacked my health, my finances, my marriage and other things. It was time to step back and reclaim that my life is God's. I had to demand that Satan take his hands off of me and what is mine. By the way, he has to pay back seven-fold of what he steals so I am here to tell you that he will not let go easily. He will hold on with all he has. I got sick of it and on my way home from work I began my reclamation (incognito for yelling at Satan) and this is how it went,

"I say in the name of Jesus Christ, Satan go back to hell where you belong, take your demons with you and get your hands off of my life! I rebuke you with the authority of the name of Jesus and as a child of the King, I bind you and your demonic spirits to leave me and my family alone! You will give me back my marriage, you will give me back my health, you will give me back my finances! You will take your hands off of my children, you will take your hands off my grandchildren, for my family belongs to God! Now that you have been made aware, you MUST pay back seven-fold of what you have stolen and I expect payment promptly! I thank you Lord God, for *your* grace is sufficient. Your power is unwavering. Go before me Lord in this battle of the spiritual attacks on me and mine. Father, let me be an even more diligent servant of you and teach me as I go. Praise your name Jesus! Praise your name!" Yes, I quoted it because I recorded it on my phone as I demanded Satan's release of me and my family and so that I do not forget it. I don't say this prayer to pump myself up, but I share it with you because I too, have to be reminded from time to time of the authority of His name. I have to be reminded that I *am* a child of God. I have to be reminded to praise Him. It is easy to praise when things are good but when things are rough, sometimes we forget the most basic thing … praising the Lord!!

Nobody ever said that spiritual warfare was easy or that you would be immune from spiritual attacks. No! Just the opposite, because Satan cannot stand that you are a warrior fighting against his demonic forces. He will come at you from every angle and will hook his claws in and hold on for dear life because he does not want to pay you back nor does he want to lose a soul to heaven. He will do everything he can to turn your focus from God so that you cannot carry out the very work the Lord is asking of you. I am here to tell you to hang on because God will rebuke the devourer as long as you remain obedient to His Word. When you find your focus trailing off, remember the thief who is coming to try to steal, kill and destroy, (John 10:10 KJV, 2012.) Satan will try to steal your mind but remember, you have the mind of Christ! I ask you to put on your armor and to bury the Word so deep in your heart that it becomes a flowering scriptural garden. This is something that takes time. It takes a lot of work on both your and God's part to make you the warrior God needs for you to be. This book is the first lesson He has for you.

We have heard forever that time is short and the thing is, it is short. We have little time left so we need to get to work! I am not predicting when Jesus is coming back but I am no fool either. I can read, and according to His Word, time is quickly coming to the finale. You must be prepared for what is coming. The demonic spirits are working overtime. Look at what is happening in our world today. Are you working overtime to send that demonic plague right back to hell? Let's keep trucking then.

God has let me know that there is more to come but for now, He needs you to know how to find Him and how to develop a relationship with Him. You can't just go do surgery without becoming a surgeon first which entails schooling. It is the same in spiritual warfare. You can't just go casting out demons without becoming a child of God and learning His techniques and requirements for casting them out. I beseech you to come to know Jesus as your personal Lord and Savior. Ask God to always put people in your path that will help you stay focused. I told you that you will need the prayer of your pastor and the congregation and I wasn't kidding. Not only will it help to keep you strong but it will help keep you safe. As the song by Sabine Baring goes … Onward Christian Soldiers.

I am pleading with you to take the basics in this lesson and begin your development and application of each piece. Only once you have become strong in God's foundation, can you move on to the next lesson. Remember the parable about building a house on the sand … I choose the rock. The chief cornerstone to build on and hope you will too.

I wish you peace, love and joy from the bottom of my heart. I ask you to remember to keep looking up to the hills from whence cometh your help (Psalm 121 KJV, 2012.)

I will close this book with a prayer from my heart.

> "Lord, I just love and thank You for all that You
> have done. I thank You for the sacrifice of Your
> son, Jesus, because You love us so much. Father,
> I just can't imagine giving up one of my children

although, they belong to You anyway. Father, I just ask that You take this book, place it in the hands of those who will use it in the way You intend. I pray that souls would first be saved for Your kingdom and that this book be used for Your edification. Let Your name be praised and lifted up! Glory to God! You are most excellent! Your will be done Father, and I pray that whoever's hands this book may be placed in, they feel the drawing of Your Holy Spirit and come to accept You in their hearts. Father for those who are to become warriors in this particular type of assignment, I pray You help them gird up and remove all fear. Pour out Your anointing, Father. Give them peace and understanding according to Your Word. Let all the works that go forth from this writing be according to Your instruction and protection. I also ask that You bind any evil, Lord, that some may try to use this book for. Father God, I give You all glory and praise! Let Your warriors prepare, and help us as we go forth with Your sword to fight against those powers and principalities of the devil. Let Your children be blessed as we endeavor to fight the enemy and expand Your kingdom oh Lord. In the name of Jesus, Amen!"

References

Holman Bible. (2012). *King James study bible*. 1st ed. Nashville: Holman Bible Pub.

Strong, J., Kohlenberger, J., Swanson, J. and Strong, J. (2001). *The strongest Strong's exhaustive concordance of the Bible*. Grand Rapids, Mich.: Zondervan.

Merriam-webster.com. (2017). *Dictionary by Merriam-Webster: America's most-trusted online dictionary*. [online] Available at: http://merriam-webster.com [Accessed 15 Apr. 2017].

AFSP. (2017). *Suicide Statistics — AFSP*. [online] Available at: https://afsp.org/about-suicide/suicide-statistics/ [Accessed 15 Apr. 2017].

Anon, (2017). [online] Available at: http://youthtoday.org/2016/06/pine-ridge-suicides-highlight-str-american-youth/ [Accessed 15 Apr. 2017].

Afterschoolsatan.com. (2017). [online] Available at: https://afterschoolsatan.com [Accessed 11 Nov. 2017].

Printed in the United States
By Bookmasters